PREACH
FOR A
YEAR #4

Books by Roger Campbell

Preach for a Year #1
Preach for a Year #2
Preach for a Year #3
Preach for a Year #4
Staying Positive in a Negative World
You Can Win!

PREACH FOR A YEAR #4

104 Sermon Outlines
Two complete outlines for every Sunday of the year

Roger Campbell

kregel
PUBLICATIONS

Grand Rapids, MI 49501

Preach for a Year #4 by Roger F. Campbell

Copyright © 1996 by Kregel Publications, a division of Kregel, Inc., P.O. Box 2607, Grand Rapids, MI 49501. Kregel Publications provides trusted, biblical publications for Christian growth and service. Your comments and suggestions are valued.

Cover photographs: Sid Lenger
Cover design: Don Ellens

Library of Congress Cataloging-in-Publication Data
Campbell, Roger F., 1930–
    Preach for a year #4 / by Roger F. Campbell.
        p.   cm.
    Includes index.
    1. Sermons—Outlines, syllabi, etc. I. Title.
BV4223.C33   1996   251'.02–dc20   87–29400
                                                            CIP
ISBN 0-8254-2329-5 (pbk., vol. 1)
ISBN 0-8254-2330-9 (pbk., vol. 2)
ISBN 0-8254-2321-x (pbk., vol. 3)
ISBN 0-8254-2318-x (pbk., vol. 4)

Printed in the United States of America
2 3 4 5 / 00 99 98 97

To pastor Wayne Otte, who first urged me to make my sermon outlines available to others.

CONTENTS

CONTENTS   9

INTRODUCTION

Thank you for opening *Preach for a Year #4*. This is not a book about preaching techniques but an invitation to come into my study and join me in preparing to preach. Your ability to develop these outlines, born in study and prayer, into sermons may be far greater than mine. Your eloquent delivery may take these helps for preaching to heights of effectiveness they have never reached before.

To God be the glory!

One minister, who had been using one of the other *Preach for a Year* books, called to thank me for my part in feeding his congregation for the past year. If *Preach for a Year #4* is helpful in feeding the sheep our Lord has entrusted to you, I will be grateful.

These are expository outlines. Leonard Ravenhill wrote: "Brother ministers, let not sin-sick souls, with burdened minds and battered spirits, turn away from our messages empty because, when they sought a spiritual remedy, we offered them only one more dreary diagnosis of the crisis of the hour!" Paul said, "Preach the Word" (2 Tim. 4:2).

Outlines are ineffective apart from heartfelt preaching. Richard Baxter urged preachers to speak often to troubled hearts, which, he said, would always assure them of an audience. His goal was to preach as if he'd never preach again and as a dying man to dying people.

These outlines have been prayerfully developed to bring people to Christ and build them up in the faith. They are pulpit tested and await greater usefulness as you use them to communicate God's message through your spiritual gifts to your congregation.

ROGER CAMPBELL

Our Timeless God

Genesis 1:1–3

I. **Introduction**
  A. *The Focus of New Year's Day*
    1. The past is past
    2. A new beginning
  B. *The Real Beginning*
    1. Creation of the universe
    2. The beginning of all we see and know
  C. *Learning About Our Creator*

II. **Body**
  A. *God Existed before Creation (v. 1)*
    1. Common sense demands something or someone eternal
      a. Must we ever ask "What was before that?"
      b. No, God has always been there
        (1) Some look back to eternal slime
        (2) We look back to our Lord divine
    2. God is eternal (Deut. 33:27)(Isa. 43:10)
      a. Look back forever and God is there (Ps. 90:2)
      b. Look ahead forever and God is there (Rev. 22:5)
    3. This is why God can offer eternal life (John 3:16; 5:24)
  B. *God Is Separate from His Creation (v. 1)*
    1. The majestic beginning of the Bible
      a. Repudiates Atheism: God exists
      b. Repudiates Pantheism: God was before His creation
    2. All things are of His design and for His glory
      a. The heavens declare His glory (Ps. 19:1)
      b. Flowers demonstrate His care (Matt. 6:28–30)
      c. The seas own Him as Master (Mark 4:39)
    3. Creation causes all people to be without excuse
      a. It preaches everywhere (Ps. 19:3)
      b. It speaks of His eternal power and Godhead (Rom. 1:20)
      c. We are all accountable to our great Creator

    C. *God's Plan for His Creation (vv. 2 & 3)*
        1. He did not leave creation in chaos (without form and void)
        2. The Holy Spirit at work to bring order and usefulness
           a. He does this in our lives
           b. Faith in Christ brings the new birth (John 3:3, 5)
           c. New life replaces the old (2 Cor. 5:17)
        3. Light instead of darkness
           a. "Let there be light"
           b. Our Lord the light of the world (John 8:12)
           c. God's Word a light for our path (Ps. 119:105)
           d. God brings light to our lives (Ps. 27:1)

III. Conclusion
    A. *Eternal Life from Our Eternal God*
        1. Escaping the restrictions of time
        2. Here our days are numbered (Ps. 90:10)
        3. Wise ones prepare for eternity (Ps. 90:12)
    B. *Receive Christ by Faith to Prepare for Eternity*
        1. Nothing can separate us from His love (Rom. 8:38–39)
        2. Trusting Jesus guarantees eternal life (I John 5:13)

The Great Annual Race

1 Corinthians 9:27
Philippians 3:13–14; Hebrews 12:1–2

I. **Introduction**
  A. *The Bible Compares the Christian Life to a Race*
    1. Each year we run another leg of the journey
    2. Each year brings us closer to the goal
  B. *All Runners Long to Win*
  C. *What Do We Need to Win the Race?*
II. **Body**
  A. *We Need Discipline (1 Cor. 9:24–27)*
    1. Astronauts said to have the right stuff
      a. They are chosen carefully
      b. They go through rigorous training
      c. They become disciplined people
    2. Believers must also be disciplined
      a. Disciplined in devotional life
      b. Disciplined in what we think
      c. Disciplined in what we say
      d. Disciplined morally
    3. We must achieve self control
      a. "Temperate in all things"
      b. This comes from the Holy Spirit (Gal. 5:21–22)
    4. We must be led by the Spirit, not by the flesh
  B. *We Need Direction (Phil. 3:13–14)*
    1. We cannot win by looking back
      a. "Forgetting those things which are behind"
      b. Leaving the past behind
      c. Forgetting old wrongs and wounds
    2. "Reaching forth unto those things which are before"
      a. Seizing opportunities to serve Christ
      b. Stretching forward with anticipation
      c. Eagerly welcoming all spiritual challenges
    3. Pressing "toward the mark"
      a. Making the best use of time for service
      b. Always living for the glory of God
      c. Always expecting the Lord's return

    4. Living with eternal rewards in mind (the prize)
    5. Rewards received at the upward calling
       (Rev. 22:12)
C. *We Need to Be Dressed for the Race (Heb. 12:1–2)*
    1. "Lay aside every weight"
      a. Runners dress lightly
      b. No extra weight to slow them down
    2. What weights have been hindering your progress?
      a. Have you been weighed down with cares?
      b. Have you been unwilling to forgive?
      c. Have you been encumbered by negativism?
      d. Have you been slowed by fears?
    3. Winners lay aside weights that drain their energy

III. Conclusion
A. *How Are You Doing in the Great Annual Race?*
B. *Rewards for Winners Will Make Every Effort Worthwhile*
C. *It Will Be Worth It All When We See Christ*

When the Body Pleases God

1 Corinthians 12:11–26

I. **Introduction**
   A. *Names of the Collective Body of Believers*
      1. The church (Acts 2:47)
      2. The bride of Christ (Eph. 5:30–32)
      3. The temple of God (Eph. 2:20–22)
      4. The body of Christ (Eph. 5:30)
   B. *Right Attitudes in the Body of Christ Please Him*
   C. *What Are These Right Attitudes?*

II. **Body**
   A. *There Is Individuality in the Body (vv. 11–17)*
      1. What we have in common
         a. All baptized by one Spirit
         b. All baptized into one body
         c. All made to drink of one Spirit
      2. What we have as individuals
         a. We retain our own temperaments
         b. We retain our own personalities
         c. Not building blocks but living stones
            (1 Peter 2:4)
      3. The Corinthian church neglected this truth
         (1 Cor. 3)
         a. Shouldn't long to be someone else
         b. Should accept ourselves as we are
   B. *There Is No Inferiority in the Body (vv. 18–22)*
      1. A bridge-verse to comfort (v. 18)
         a. God has set us in the body
         b. We are gifted as it pleases Him
      2. We must accept ourselves and others
      3. We need each other
         a. We are not all the same
         b. We compliment one another
         c. Serving together we please our Lord
      4. The feeble members are needed too (vv. 22–24)
         a. No one to be looked down on
         b. Honor enough for all

C. *There Is to Be Intimate Fellowship in the Body*
   (vv. 25–26)
1. "There should be no schism in the body"
2. We are to care for one another
3. We are to love one another
4. We are to respond when another member suffers
5. We are to rejoice when another member is honored
6. We are not to be divided but of one accord
   (Acts 2:1)

III. **Conclusion**
A. *What Happens When We Function As a Body?*
   1. Consider the first century church
   2. Thousands converted; churches established
B. *Could This Happen Today?*
C. *Why Not?*
D. *Why Not Here?*
E. *Why Not Now?*

Let's Have Harmony in the Church

Philippians 2:1–8

I. **Introduction**
   A. *When Believers Were of One Accord*
      1. They prayed with great faith (Acts. 1:14)
      2. They preached with great power (Acts 2:1)
      3. They enjoyed great fellowship (Acts 2:41–46)
      4. They experienced great growth (Acts 2:47)
   B. *Paul Challenges the Philippian Church to Be of One Accord*
      1. If there is any consolation in Christ
      2. If there is any comfort of love
      3. If there is any fellowship of the Spirit
      4. If you have any affection and mercy
   C. *How to Have Harmony in a Church*

II. **Body**
   A. *Let Nothing Be Done through Strife or Vainglory (v. 3)*
      1. Ending strife gives a church new life
      2. Strife keeps bad company
         a. Joined with envy, divisions, carnality (1 Cor. 3:3)
         b. Named with the works of the flesh (Gal. 5:19–21)
         c. Comes from Satan (James 3:14–16)
      3. Service to glorify the servant is worthless
      4. All work in the church should glorify God (Col. 3:23)
   B. *Let Each Esteem Others Better Than Themselves (v. 3)*
      1. Here is a different dimension to self-esteem
         a. The great push for self-esteem
         b. Paul calls for higher esteem for others
      2. Esteem for others grows out of love
         a. Love enables us to forget the faults of others
         b. When you build on a fault expect an earthquake
         c. Love enables us to look for the best in others
      3. This esteem causes us to care for the needs of others (v. 4)

        a. Our concern for them is greater than for ourselves

        b. We want to protect them and what is dear to them

C. *Let This Mind Be in You, Which Was Also in Christ Jesus (v. 5)*

    1. Here is the key to heeding Paul's call

        a. How to put away strife and vainglory

        b. How to esteem others better than ourselves

        c. How to care more for the things of others than of our own

    2. The mind of Christ conquers carnality

        a. Makes us humble instead of hateful

        b. Makes us giving instead of greedy

        c. Makes us selfless instead of selfish

    3. We learn about the mind of Christ at the cross

        a. He laid aside His glory; how can we seek glory?

        b. He humbled Himself; how can we be proud?

        c. He became a servant; how can we covet high positions?

        d. He was obedient to death; how can we do less?

III. Conclusion

    A. *Exaltation Follows Humility (vv. 9–10)*

    B. *A Humble, Caring Church, Will Be a United Church*

    C. *A United Church Will Be Effective in Its Ministry*

Hiding from God

Genesis 3:8

I. **Introduction**
   A. *One of the Most Basic Chapters in the Bible*
      1. Records the temptation and fall (vv. 1–6)
      2. Promises redemption (v. 15)
   B. *God Walks in the Garden in the Cool of the Day*
      1. It is time for sweet fellowship with Him
      2. Adam and Eve have gone into hiding
   C. *People Are Still Hiding from God*

II. **Body**
   A. *Some Hide from God at the Time of His Investigation*
      1. "Where art thou?"
      2. God is always seeking sinners
         a. Jesus came to seek and save the lost (Luke 19:10)
         b. Conviction of sin is evidence God is seeking
         c. God speaking through His Word shows He is seeking
         d. Sometimes He seeks through trials
         e. Sometimes He seeks through preachers
         f. Sometimes He seeks through caring friends
      3. Hiding from God is futile (Ps. 139)
         a. There is no place to hide from Him
         b. Even darkness cannot hide us (vv. 11–12)
   B. *Some Hide from God at the Time of His Invitation*
      1. "Ye will not come to me that ye might have life" (John 5:40)
      2. The most difficult hiding to understand
      3. Our Lord's invitation goes out to all
         a. The tender truth of John 3:16
         b. The compassion of the Cross
      4. Our Lord's gracious invitations
         a. "Come unto me" (Matt. 11:28)
         b. The last invitation in the Bible: "Come" (Rev. 22:17)
      5. Adam and Eve hiding among the trees
      6. Trees people hide behind today:

        a. Busy schedules, hypocrites, other excuses
        b. Nothing changes (Luke 14:16–24)

C. *Some Will Hide from God at the Time of His*
    Indignation (Rev. 6:16)
    1. The wrath of the Lamb
        a. How strange: an angry Lamb!
        b. The Lamb slain on the cross
    2. Jesus is the Lamb
        a. He came to take away the sin of the world
        b. He came to deliver us from wrath (John 3:36)
    3. Identifying those trying to hide
        a. The kings of the earth (position makes no
            difference)
        b. Chief captains and mighty men (power doesn't
            protect)
        c. All who are free and slaves (riches do not
            save)

III. Conclusion
    A. *Safety Comes from Hiding in Christ Now*
        1. Hidden with Christ in God (Col. 3:1–3)
        2. Cannot hide from Him but can hide in Him
    B. *Respond to God's Call and Come Out of Hiding*
    C. *Come to Him and Be Safe*

What Have You Done?

Genesis 3:13

I. **Introduction**
   A. *The First Question God Ever Asked a Woman*
      1. After she had eaten of the forbidden fruit
      2. After she had shared her sin with her husband
   B. *Considering God's Searching Question to Eve*

II. **Body**
   A. *A Question about Life's Most Serious Subject*
      1. The subject is sin
      2. God's original warning: death
         a. Came when they were in a perfect environment
         b. Came when they enjoyed perfect fellowship
         c. Everything else in the garden was for them
      3. Today's testimonies to the truth of God's warning
         a. Every siren and every hospital
         b. Every funeral and every cemetery
         c. Every sign of advancing age
         d. Every crime and act of violence
      4. Eve needed to know the seriousness of her act
      5. God's question drives His point home
   B. *It Is a Question That Calls for Repentance*
      1. "What is this that thou hast done?"
         a. It is a specific question
         b. It is a pointed question
         c. It is a stern question
         d. It is a question that demands personal investigation
      2. God's questions are not to condemn but to convict
      3. Conviction of sin brings repentance
         a. Repentance begins with awareness of sin
         b. Repentance is a change of attitude about sin
      4. How would you answer God's question to Eve?
         a. What have you done?
         b. What brings conviction to your heart?
         c. What do you need to confess and forsake?
      5. Turn from your sins to Christ
      6. God is not willing that any perish (2 Peter 3:9)

    C. It Is a Question That Precedes the Promise of
        Redemption
      1. Bruising the serpent's head (v. 15)
        a. This is the first promise of redemption
        b. Christ bruised the serpent's head at the cross
        c. Redemption made possible for you and me
      2. Like Eve, we are all sinners (Rom. 3:23)
        a. We have all done things we regret
        b. We have all broken God's laws
        c. Not one of us is righteous
      3. God offers forgiveness and eternal life to sinners
      4. Whatever you have done, God loves you
        a. Bring your sins to Him
        b. Place your faith in Him (Rom. 5:1)
        c. His grace is sufficient to save

III. Conclusion
    A. Hear God's Question Again: "What Is This Thou Hast
       Done?"
    B. Respond to God's Loving Invitation and Be Born
       Again (John 3:16)

Groaning Now . . . Glory Later

Romans 8:18

I. Introduction
  A. *Riches in Romans Eight*
    1. A chapter of hope, comfort, strength, anticipation
    2. Begins with two wonderful words: "NO CONDEMNATION"
  B. *Good Things for Those Who Are Not Condemned*
    1. They are the sons of God (vv. 14–15)
    2. They are joint heirs with Christ (v. 17)
    3. They are going to be glorified with Christ (v. 19)
    4. All things work together for their good (v. 28)
    5. God's plan is to make them more like Jesus (v. 29)
    6. They can never be separated from God's love (vv. 38–39)
  C. *A Special Promise for Believers Who Suffer*

II. Body
  A. *There Is Suffering Now*
    1. All experience suffering to some degree
    2. Every hospital shouts: *"There is suffering now"*
    3. Every siren adds its wail in the night
    4. Both physical and emotional suffering
       a. Some suffering is brought on us by others
       b. We bring some suffering on ourselves
    5. Paul knew what it was to suffer
       a. He had gone without food
       b. He had been in storms and shipwrecks
       c. He had been whipped and stoned for his faith
       d. He suffered from a "thorn in the flesh"
    6. The sufferings of Jesus for us all
  B. *There Will Be Glory Later*
    1. The best is yet to come
    2. "I go to prepare a place for you" (John 14:1–3)
    3. To depart and be with Christ is far better (Phil. 1:21–23)
    4. Some things about heaven
       a. A place of music (Rev. 5:9)
       b. A place of praise (Rev. 7:9–12)

    c. A place of service (Rev. 7:13–15)
    d. A place of comfort (Rev. 7:16–17)
    e. A place of rest (Rev. 14:13)
    f. A place of rejoicing (Rev. 19:7)
    g. No sickness, sorrow, or death there
        (Rev. 21:1–6)

C. *The Suffering Now Cannot Be Compared to the Glory Later*

   1. The rapture of the church is ahead (1 Thess. 4:13–18)
   2. Rewards are ahead (Rev. 22:12)
   3. The Kingdom is ahead (Rev. 19)
   4. Earthly suffering is only for a time
   5. Glory is for eternity

III. Conclusion

A. *Are You Suffering Now?*

B. *Could Your Suffering Be Designed to Bring You to Jesus?*

C. *Christ Will Meet You in Your Suffering*

D. *Receive Him by Faith and Be Sure of Glory Later*

The Preacher's Pay and Fringe Benefits

1 Corinthians 9:1–18

I. **Introduction**
  A. *Money Is Always a Sensitive Subject*
      1. Especially true in the church
      2. Some think money should never be mentioned
      3. Paul taught believers about money
          a. To give regularly and systematically (1 Cor. 16:2)
          b. To give as the Lord has given (1 Cor. 16:2)
          c. To give cheerfully (2 Cor. 9:7)
          d. To provide for the needs of the preacher (1 Cor. 9)
  B. *Why Should a Preacher Be Paid?*

II. **Body**
  A. *The Bible Basis of the Preacher's Pay (vv. 1–14)*
      1. Logical questions about the preacher's pay
          a. Do we not have the right to refrain from work? (v. 6)
          b. Who goes to war and pays his own way? (v. 7)
          c. Who plants a vineyard and can't eat the grapes? (v. 7)
          d. Who feeds a flock and can't drink the milk? (v. 7)
      2. Lessons from the law about the preacher's pay
          a. Don't muzzle the ox that treads the corn (v. 9)
          b. Those who plow expect a crop (v. 10)
          c. Those who reap should share in the harvest (v. 10)
          d. Temple workers received part of the offerings (v. 13)
      3. Spiritual sowing should bring material reaping (v. 11)
      4. Those who preach the gospel should be paid for it (v. 14)
  B. *The Preacher's Pay Should Never Affect His Preaching (vv. 12–16)*
      1. Paul and his associates often went without pay

      a. They deserved pay but didn't receive it
      b. This didn't stop them from preaching
    2. They let nothing "hinder" the gospel
      a. Wealthy donors were not favored
      b. Sermon subjects were not affected
      c. The gospel was not compromised
      d. Pay or no pay they preached the Gospel
    3. God's will must be carried out regardless of pay
      a. Money must not influence the preacher
      b. God provides for His servants
  C. *The Preacher's Pay Is on Its Way (vv. 17–19)*
    1. Rewards await faithful preachers of the gospel
      a. Even if there is no pay here
      b. God will reward His servants
    2. God's plan calls for His servants to be paid
      a. If not paid, He will reward them
      b. Sustenance now somehow and rewards to come
    3. Paul's anticipated rewards
      a. The crown of rejoicing (his converts) (1 Thess. 2:19)
      b. The crown of righteousness (2 Tim. 4:8)
    4. Our Lord's "Well done!" will be reward enough

III. Conclusion
  A. *God's Plan Is for a Church to Pay Its Preacher*
    1. In doing so they share in his rewards
    2. In doing so they free him for greater service
  B. *Preachers Must Preach the Gospel*
    1. Ideally, with the support of the churches
    2. If not, with confidence their Lord will provide

I Am the Bread of Life

"I Am" Series Begins   *John 6:35*

I. **Introduction**
   A. *Introducing the "I Am" Series*
      1. Moses and the "I AM" revelation (Exod. 3:14)
      2. Jesus shocks His hearers:
         a. "Before Abraham was, I am" (John 8:58)
         b. His enemies then wanted to stone Him
   B. *The Eight "I Am" Statements by Jesus*
      1. Seven in the Gospel of John
      2. One in the Book of Revelation
   C. *The First "I Am" Declaration: I Am the Bread of Life*
      1. What does this statement mean?
      2. How does it apply to us today?

II. **Body**
   A. *Jesus Is the Source of Life*
      1. "All things were made by him" (John 1:3)
         a. All plant and animal life
         b. All human life (Gen. 1:26–31)
         c. "In him was life" (John 1:4)
      2. The high regard for life in the Bible
      3. Today's departure from that position
         a. Abortion: ending life before God's time for birth
         b. Euthanasia: ending life before God's time for death
      4. Life is from the Lord and should be sacred
   B. *Jesus Is the Sustainer of Life*
      1. Bread (food) is vital to sustain life
         a. No one strong enough to live long without food
         b. When food runs out life soon ends
         c. Anorexic victims die because they refuse to eat
      2. God provides food for life
         a. Israel given manna in the desert
         b. Elijah sustained by a widow during a famine
      3. Jesus gives and sustains eternal life
         a. Born in Bethlehem, the "place of bread" (Micah 5:2)

           b. Communion bread symbolizes His broken body (1 Cor. 11:24)

      4. How to receive this bread of life
           a. "He that cometh to me"
           b. All who come to Him receive salvation

  C. *Jesus Gives Satisfaction in Life*
      1. "Shall never hunger"
      2. Christ satisfies all inner desires
           a. All other sources fail to satisfy
           b. Wealth, fame, success all fail
      3. Jesus also satisfies inner thirst (shall never thirst)
           a. Inner thirst sends some to alcohol and other drugs
           b. Inner thirst sends some to lust and greed
           c. None of these satisfy
      4. True satisfaction is found only in Jesus

III. **Conclusion**
  A. *Coming and Believing*
      1. Easy to understand
      2. No complicated religious ceremonies
  B. *Come to Christ and Have Life*

I Am the Light of the World

"I Am" Series   *John 8:1–12*

I. **Introduction**
   A. *The "I Am" Series*
      1. Jesus reveals Himself as the eternal Son of God
      2. The "I AM" statements help us understand Him
   B. *The Light of the World*
      1. What does this "I AM" statement mean?
      2. How does it relate to you and me?

II. **Body**
   A. *Light Brings a Knowledge of Our Need (vv. 1–9)*
      1. "Then" (v. 12) refers to the previous experience
      2. The woman taken in adultery
      3. All eyes focused on this guilty woman
      4. The Pharisees attempt to catch Jesus between law and grace
         a. He said He had come to fulfill the law
         b. He was also the friend of sinners
         c. The law demanded death for adultery
         d. What would Jesus do?
      5. Jesus stooped and wrote on the ground
         a. The law had been written in stone for Moses
         b. Perhaps he wrote the Commandments in the sand
         c. The law makes us all face our sins
      6. The Pharisees now made aware of their sins
         a. "Let him . . . cast the first stone"
         b. Exposed to the light they all departed
   B. *Light Brings Hope to the Hopeless (v. 10)*
      1. The woman was guilty, without hope
      2. Now she would have hope, forgiveness
         a. "Where are thine accusers?"
         b. "Neither do I condemn thee"
      3. Light for all in the dark
         a. The dayspring from on high (Luke 1:78)
         b. A light for the Gentiles (Luke 2:32)
         c. The light was the life of men (John 1:4–6)
      4. Our Lord's passion for a lost world

31

      a. "World" appears 77 times in John's Gospel
      b. Capsulized in John 3:16
   5. The adulteress deserved death but received life
   6. She deserved to be condemned but received pardon

C. *Light Brings Direction to Those Who Are Delivered*
     (vv. 11–12)
   1. "Go, and sin no more"
   2. "Shall not walk in darkness, but shall have the light of life"
   3. These are directions for those who have been forgiven
      a. Salvation is only the beginning (Eph. 2:8–10)
      b. We are not to walk in darkness anymore
      c. We are to walk in newness of life (Rom. 6:4)

III. **Conclusion**
   A. *The Sinless Savior Brings Light and Life to Sinners*
   B. *Come Out of Darkness to the Light of the World*
   C. *He Will Enable You to Walk in His Light*

I Am the Door

"I Am" Series   *John 10:7–10*

I. **Introduction**
   A. *Jesus Taught Great Spiritual Truths Simply*
      1. I am the bread of life
      2. I am the light of the world
   B. *How Clearly He Explained the Deep Things of God*
      1. "I am the door of the sheep" (v. 7)
      2. A simple salvation message for sinners

II. **Body**
   A. *Christ Is the Door (v. 7)*
      1. A door is for exiting and entering
      2. Christ is the door to forgiveness
         a. Those who trust Him exit condemnation (John 3:17)
         b. Those who trust Him enter justification (Rom. 5:1)
      3. Christ is the door to life
         a. Those who trust Him exit spiritual death (Eph. 2:1)
         b. Those who trust Him enter a new life (2 Cor. 5:17)
      4. Christ is the door to heaven
         a. Those who trust Him exit the road to hell (John 3:36)
         b. Those who trust Him enter eternal life (John 5:24)
      5. Have you entered eternal life?
         a. Eternal life is a present possession (1 John 5:12)
         b. We can know we have eternal life now (1 John 5:13)
   B. *Christ Is the Only Door (v. 8)*
      1. There is no other door to forgiveness
      2. There is no other door to new life
      3. There is no other door to heaven
      4. There is no other door to eternal life
      5. Many try to find other doors

        a. Religious doors: baptism, communion, church membership
        b. Financial doors: giving to churches or charities
        c. Doors of personal merit: good works, honesty, etc.
        d. Cultic doors: false Christs (v. 8), false doctrines
    6. All of these fail: Christ alone is the door (Acts 4:12)

C. *Christ Is the Door for All Who Believe (v. 9)*
    1. "If any man enter in"
        a. The invitation is open to all
        b. Another way to say "whosoever" (John 3:16; Rom. 10:13)
    2. This door opens for all who wish to enter
        a. It opens for all sinners (Rom. 3:23; 5:8)
        b. It opens for all who come to Jesus (John 6:37)
        c. It opens for all races (Rom. 10:12)
    3. Those who enter this door find salvation
        a. "Shall be saved"
        b. No doubt about it
    4. Those who enter this door are in the sheepfold
    5. Those who enter this door are satisfied, "find pasture"

III. Conclusion
    A. *Reject All Falsely Labeled Doors*
    B. *Come to Christ As You Are, a Sinner*
    C. *Christ Awaits You: Don't Delay!*

I Am the Good Shepherd

"I Am" Series   *John 10:11*

I. **Introduction**
   A. *The Tenderest of All the "I Am" Statements*
      1. As the Bread of Life, He satisfies
      2. As the Light of the World, He sanctifies
      3. As the Door, He saves
      4. As the Good Shepherd, He reveals who He is
   B. *Getting to Know the Good Shepherd*

II. **Body**
   A. *As the Good Shepherd, Jesus Reveals His Character*
      1. The prophets knew the Lord as the good shepherd
         a. David: "The LORD" is my shepherd (Ps. 23)
         b. Isaiah: "He shall feed His flock like a shepherd (40:11)
         c. Ezekiel: "I will search for my sheep" (34:11–16)
      2. The "Good" Shepherd
         a. The Lord is good (Nahum 1:7)
         b. Only one is good (Matt. 19:16–17)
         c. This then reveals the deity of Christ
      3. Three New Testament titles of Christ the shepherd:
         a. The good Shepherd dying for His sheep (John 10:11)
         b. The great Shepherd risen for His sheep (Heb. 13:20)
         c. The chief Shepherd coming for His sheep (1 Peter 5:4)
      4. We can know this good Shepherd as our own
   B. *As the Good Shepherd, Jesus Reveals His Care*
      1. The good Shepherd speaks to His sheep (v. 3)
      2. The good Shepherd calls His sheep by name (v. 3)
      3. The good Shepherd leads His sheep (v. 3)
      4. The good Shepherd goes before His sheep (v. 4)
      5. The good Shepherd protects His sheep (v. 12)
      6. The good Shepherd stays with His sheep (v. 13)
      7. The good Shepherd gives eternal life to His sheep (vv. 27–29)

    C. As the Good Shepherd, Jesus Reveals His Cross
      1. Laying down His life for His sheep (v. 15)
        a. Here is the cross with all its suffering
        b. Voluntarily dying for His sheep
      2. Providing salvation for all His sheep
        a. Salvation for the "other sheep" (Gentiles) (v. 16)
        b. Jews and Gentiles both need salvation
        c. Jews and Gentiles can be saved (Rom. 10:12–13)
      3. Conquering death for His sheep (vv. 17–18)
        a. The cross was in the Father's plan
        b. "No man taketh it from me"
        c. "Power to take it again" (Resurrection)
      4. Giving eternal life to His sheep (v. 28)
      5. Securely holding His sheep (v. 28)
      6. Guaranteeing the future of His sheep (v. 28)

III. Conclusion
    A. Do You Know the Good Shepherd As Your Own?
    B. Do You Wonder If He Really Loves You?
      1. Consider the Cross
      2. Stop doubting His love
    C. Come to the Good Shepherd by Faith Today

I Am the Resurrection and the Life

I. **Introduction**
   A. *Who Is Jesus Christ?*
      1. Let Him answer the question
         a. I am the bread of life (John 6:35)
         b. I am the light of the world (John 8:12)
         c. I am the door (John 10:9)
         d. I am the good Shepherd (John 10:11)
      2. Four more "I AM" statements to follow
   B. *The Resurrection and the Life*
      1. What can we learn from this amazing statement?
      2. How can we apply it to our lives?

II. **Body**
   A. *Jesus Is the Greatest of All Personalities (v. 25)*
      1. What led to this moving scene?
         a. Declaring His deity: "I and my Father are one" (10:29)
         b. The enemies of Jesus tried to kill Him
         c. Jesus ministered beyond Jordan, having many converts
         d. A message arrived that Lazarus was sick (11:1)
         e. Jesus waited two days before leaving for Bethany (11:6)
         f. The disciples learned that Lazarus was dead (v. 14)
      2. Grieving Martha and our Lord's response
         a. "If thou hadst been here" (v. 21)
         b. "Thy brother will rise again" (v. 23)
      3. Things will turn out better than Martha thinks
      4. Jesus is always up to the occasion
   B. *Jesus Holds the Greatest of All Powers (v. 25)*
      1. "Though he were dead, yet shall he live"
      2. Take it literally, Martha!
         a. Martha had staggered at His earlier promise (v. 23)
         b. She thinks He is talking about the coming resurrection

      c. Martha limits the Lord's promise
      d. Even so, His promise would be fulfilled
  3. True, Lazarus will rise in the resurrection
  4. All believers will rise at the rapture
      (1 Thess. 4:13–18)
  5. He would also be raised then as the Lord promised
  6. Jesus has power to raise the dead, the greatest power

C. *Jesus Extends the Greatest of All Promises (v. 26)*
  1. "Shall never die"
  2. Life is short at its longest
      a. According to the psalmist, 70 to 80 years
      b. We're still in that range today
  3. Jesus promises life that lasts: everlasting life
  4. Everlasting life is better than 70 or 80 years . . . or 100 years
  5. Everlasting life is ours through faith in Christ

III. Conclusion
  A. *Do You Know the Greatest Person?*
  B. *Are You Resting in His Great Power?*
  C. *Are You Trusting His Great Promises?*
  D. *Do You Now Possess Everlasting Life?*

I Am the Way, the Truth, and the Life

I. **Introduction**
   A. *Jesus Prepares the Disciples for His Departure (chap. 13)*
      1. The last Passover before His death
      2. Washing the feet of His disciples
      4. Breaking bread together
      5. Revealing His coming betrayal
   B. *The Promise of Heaven*
      1. "Let not your heart be troubled"
      2. Many mansions in His Father's house
      3. "I go to prepare a place for you"
   C. *The "I Am" to Answer a Disciple's Question*
      1. How can we know the way?
      2. A good question for us all

II. **Body**
   A. *Jesus Is the Way to Heaven*
      1. Not, "I will show you the way"
      2. Not, "Here is the way"
      3. You cannot follow Jesus to heaven
         a. He was baptized, but you can be baptized and lost
         b. He loved people, but you can love people and be lost
         c. He was a man of prayer, but you can pray and be lost
      4. Salvation comes through faith in Christ
         a. "Whosoever believeth in Him" (John 3:16)
         b. "Believe on the Lord Jesus Christ" (Acts 16:31)
         c. "By grace are ye saved through faith" (Eph. 2:8)
         d. "Therefore being justified by faith" (Rom. 5:1)
   B. *Jesus Is the Source of Truth about Heaven*
      1. There are many errors about heaven
         a. Some think heaven is on earth
         b. Some think only 144,000 will go to heaven
         c. Some think heaven is a state of mind

   2. Some truth about heaven from Jesus
      a. Heaven is a place (v. 2)
      b. Heaven is a prepared place (v. 2)
      c. Heaven is where Christians go at death (v. 3)
      d. Heaven is where Jesus will take us when He
         comes (v. 3)
   3. We can depend on the words Jesus gave us about
      heaven
   C. *Jesus Is the Source of Life That Continues in Heaven*
      1. "I am the life"
         a. "In Him was life" (John 1:4)
         b. "I am the bread of life" (John 6:35)
         c. "I am the resurrection and the life"
            (John 11:25)
      2. Life is precious
         a. The loss of this truth in our time
         b. Abortion, assisted suicide, euthanasia
         c. Each moment of life is priceless
      3. Only Jesus provides life that lasts forever

III. Conclusion
   A. *Jesus Is the Only Way to Heaven*
   B. *Jesus Reveals the Truth about Heaven*
   C. *Jesus Gives Life That Continues in Heaven*
   D. *Come in Faith to Jesus and Be Sure of Heaven*

I Am the True Vine

"I Am" Series   *John 15:1–8*

I. **Introduction**
   A. *Who Is Jesus?*
      1. The question we're pursuing in the "I AM" series
      2. A question Jesus answered for His disciples
   B. *What We've Learned from His Answers*
      1. Jesus is the bread of life and the light of the world
      2. Jesus is the door to heaven and the good Shepherd
      3. Jesus is the resurrection and the life
      4. Jesus is the way, the truth, and the life
      5. Now we learn that Jesus is the true vine
   C. *The True Vine, the Husbandman, and the Branches*

II. **Body**
   A. *The True Vine (v. 1)*
      1. "I am the true vine"
      2. Other uses of "true" in the Bible
         a. The true light (John 1:9)
            (1) Jesus compared to John the Baptist
            (2) John bore witness to Jesus
            (3) Prophets and preachers can but reflect His light
         b. The true bread (John 6:32)
            (1) Jesus compared to manna
            (2) Manna provided temporal life
            (3) Jesus provides eternal life
      3. The vine provides life to the branches
      4. Christ is our source of life (John 14:6)
      5. Christ gives abundant life (John 10:10)
   B. *The True Vine in Relation to the Father (vv. 1–3)*
      1. "My father is the husbandman"
         a. The Father is the farmer
         b. The Father expects fruit
      2. The fruit of the Spirit (Gal. 5:22–23)
         a. Inward: love, joy, peace
         b. Outward: longsuffering, gentleness, goodness, faith (faithfulness), meekness (gentleness), temperance (self-control)

    3.   Fruit produced by soul winning (Prov. 11:30)
    4.   The Father prunes His vineyard
        a.   Some branches are taken away (through death)
        b.   Some branches are purged to become more fruitful
            (1)   Purged by trimming away the unnecessary
            (2)   Purged by applying the Scriptures (v. 3)

C. *The True Vine in Relation to the Branches (vv. 4–8)*
    1.   "Ye are the branches" (v. 5)
    2.   Branches let the life of the vine flow to the fruit
    3.   To bear fruit we must abide in Christ
        a.   To abide in Christ is to communicate with Him
        b.   To abide in Christ is to love Him
        c.   To abide in Christ is to praise Him
        d.   To abide in Him is to be faithful to Him
    4.   In bearing fruit we honor our Lord (v. 8)

III. **Conclusion**
    A. *Without Christ We Can Do Nothing (v . 5)*
    B. *With Christ We Bear Fruit and Glorify Our Father*

I Am Alpha and Omega

Revelation 1:8

I. Introduction

A. *The "I Am" Series Began with the Call of Moses (Exod. 3:13)*
1. Moses: "What shall I say?"
2. The Lord: "Tell them that 'I AM' hath sent you."

B. *Jesus Came Announcing Himself As the "I Am"*
1. "Before Abraham was, I Am"
2. We've learned about the Eternal One in simple terms
   a. Bread, light, the door, the good Shepherd
   b. The resurrection and the life
   c. The way, the truth, the life; the true vine

C. *Completing the Series . . . In Revelation*

II. Body

A. *The Alpha and Omega*
1. The complete One; everything we need is in Him
2. Alpha and Omega, the first and last letters of the alphabet
3. Christ says "I am the A and Z"
4. Every desire and need can be expressed in the alphabet
5. Great authors and their works
   a. All have used but the letters of the alphabet
   b. Drama, romance, history, dreams of the future
6. What could be more expressive than the alphabet?
   a. The lover makes it the vehicle of love
   b. The poet expresses unforgettable thoughts in song
7. Is your problem s–i–n, f–e–a–r, d–o–u–b–t?
8. If you can spell it, you can tell it to Jesus
9. Another way of saying: "Christ is all" (Col. 3:11)

B. *The Beginning and the End*
1. The Creator and the Judge
2. Our Lord is the great beginner and finisher
   a. Creation finished (Gen. 2:1)
      (1) Bringing order out of chaos

            (2)   Creating plants and animals
            (3)   Creating Adam and Eve
      b. Redemption finished (John 19:30)
            (1)   Prophecies of the coming Redeemer
            (2)   The birth of Jesus in Bethlehem
            (3)   The ministry of Jesus
            (4)   The death and resurrection of Jesus
      c. Some finishing awaits His return
   3. He also finishes His work in our lives (Phil. 1:6)
      a. Salvation is just the beginning
      b. He is not through with us yet (Eph. 2:10)

C. *The One Who Is to Come*
   1. "Which is, and which was, and which is to come"
   2. The One who died and rose again will come again
   3. What will happen when He comes?
      a. The dead in Christ will rise (1 Thess. 4:13–16)
      b. Living believers will be caught up
         (1 Thess. 4:17)
      c. Unbelievers will be left for the Tribulation
   4. Are you looking for the One who is to come?

III. Conclusion
   A. *We've Been Learning about a Loving All Sufficient Savior*
   B. *Do You Know Him As Your Own?*
   C. *Come to Him in Faith and Find Him All You Need*

Love Is the Greatest

1 Corinthians 13:13

I. Introduction
  A. *Love Is in God's Plan*
  1. "There is a time to love" (Eccles. 3:8)
  2. Love is greater than faith or hope (v. 13)
  B. *The Greatest Subject in the Bible*
  1. A subject that affects all people
  2. A subject that has life changing power
  a. Power to change your attitude
  b. Power to change your marriage
  c. Power to change your church
  d. Power to change your future

II. Body
  A. *God's Love for Us (1 John 4:10)*
  1. The greatest news: God loves us!
  2. The Bible is God's love letter to us all
  3. God loved us while we were sinners (Rom. 5:8)
  4. God loved us when we didn't love Him (v. 10)
  5. God's love sent Jesus to the cross (John 3:16)
  6. We will never be separated from God's love (Rom. 8:38–39)
  B. *God's Love in Our Hearts (Rom. 5:5)*
  1. "The love of God is shed abroad in our hearts"
  2. God's love then should flow through us to others
  a. Jesus loved those who were difficult to love
  b. His enemies criticized Him for loving sinners
  3. How to recognize the love of Christ in us (vv. 4–8)
  a. Love is patient and kind
  b. Love is neither touchy nor angry
  c. Love is never selfish
  d. Love is quick to forgive, doesn't hold grudges
  e. Love looks for the best in others
  C. *God's Love in the Harvest (1 Cor. 13:1)*
  1. We are to love lost people
  2. Jesus calls us to go to a lost world with His love
  a. "Go ye therefore and teach all nations" (Matt. 28:18–20)
  b. "Ye shall be my witnesses" (Acts 1:8)

    3. All going and witnessing is ineffective without love (13:1)
- a. Preaching without love is just noise
- b. Witnessing without love is worthless
- c. Giving without love is a bad investment

    4. Reaching out in love brings results
- a. Love reaches more people than logic
- b. Love reaches more people than tact
- c. Love reaches more people than training
- d. Love reaches more people than good arguments

    5. We must love people as they are
- a. This is how Jesus loved
- b. His love can make them what they ought to be

III. Conclusion

    A. *When You Don't Feel Loved*
1. Consider the Cross
2. The cross proves God's love for us

    B. *Ask the Christ of the Cross to Love Others Through You*

God Took Him

Genesis 5:24

I. **Introduction**
    A. *Introduced to a Man on the Obituary Page*
        1. A man who speaks of life in a chapter of death
        2. A gem among the genealogies
    B. *Enoch: the Man Who Did Not Die (Heb. 11:5)*
        1. "God took him" (translated that he should not see death)
        2. He was taken in the strength of his life
        3. He was taken when comparatively young
        4. His family must have missed this good man
    C. *Comfort from Enoch's Experience When Loved Ones Are Taken in Death*

II. **Body**
    A. *His Reputation before He Was Taken*
        1. He walked with God
        2. He pleased God (Heb. 11:5)
            a. He was a man of faith
            b. His life demonstrated his faith
        3. He was a prophet (Jude 14)
            a. He prophesied of the second coming of Christ
            b. He warned of coming judgment
            c. He spoke out boldly against sin
        4. Enoch's neighbors knew him as a man of God
    B. *The Reason He Was Taken*
        1. We can only speculate
            a. We know he lived in a difficult time
            b. The world was ripening for judgment
            c. God may have chosen to spare him much grief
        2. We cannot be sure why Enoch was taken
            a. We can be sure our Lord loved him
            b. We can be sure our Lord knows the future
            c. We can be sure our Lord does all things well
        3. Some things from which believers are spared at death
            a. The sorrows that are ahead
            b. The ravages of disease
            c. The infirmities of the flesh

    4. Only the Lord knows the reasons loved ones are taken

    5. We must leave the mystery of His will to Him

  C. *His Residence After He Was Taken*

    1. Enoch was taken to be with the Lord

    2. Enoch's address became heaven

    3. Christians are taken to heaven when they die

      a. They go there immediately (2 Cor. 5:8)

      b. They go to the promised mansions (John 14:1–3)

      c. They go to a place that is far better (Phil. 1:21–23)

    4. Enoch had no more human limitations after he was taken

    5. What Enoch may have seen

      a. Things he had learned about on his walks

      b. Things that surpassed all of his dreams

III. Conclusion

  A. *When God Took Enoch He Was Ready to Go*

  B. *Jesus Made It Possible for All to Be Ready to Go*

  C. *Are You Ready?*

Who Will Believe?

Series on the Cross Begins   *Isaiah 53:1–3*

I. Introduction

    A. Isaiah's Prophecy of Christ That Begins with Two Questions

        1. "Who hath believed our report?"

        2. "To whom is the arm of the Lord revealed?

    B. Two Questions That Call for Faith

        1. Who will believe because God's Word declares it?

        2. Who will believe in spite of the circumstances?

    C. Why People Would Reject the Coming Savior

II. Body

    A. The Tender Plant (v. 2)

        1. "He shall grow up before him like a tender plant"

        2. A prophecy of the coming Christ

        3. What a description of Jesus!

            a. The miracle of the incarnation

            b. His entrance into the world as a baby (Luke 2:1–20)

            c. Growing up in a family (Luke 2:40–52)

        4. Tenderness would always be a part of His life

            a. He had time for little children

            b. Lepers and other outcasts came to Him

            c. He received the broken, the sad, the sinful

        5. Tears revealed his tender heart

    B. The Root Out of Dry Ground

        1. "Like a root out of a dry ground"

        2. Israel seemed so unlikely to produce Him

            a. They had stoned the prophets and refused their message

            b. They had become subjects of the Roman Empire

            c. They had become outcasts among the nations

            d. But the Scriptures declared they would produce the Savior

        3. When Jesus came he was born of poor parents

        4. He came out of Nazareth

            a. Even the Jews struggled with this

            b. Nothing good was expected out of Nazareth (John 1:46)

       c. No prophets had come out of that area
         (John 7:52)
    5. Still, Jesus came from Nazareth and was the
      promised Savior
  C. *The Unlovely Christ*
    1. A surprising description of Christ
    2. "He hath no form nor comeliness (majesty)"
       a. No splendid surroundings
       b. No regal pomp nor splendor (Pulpit
         Commentary)
       c. The Jews were expecting a king . . . not a
         servant
    3. "No beauty that we should desire him"
       a. Nothing showy about Christ
       b. We still know nothing of His physical
         appearance
    4. To understand this verse look before and after it
       a. This is a scene from the cross (52:14 and 53:3–5)
       b. Nothing beautiful about the cross
       c. The nails, the thorns, the blood, the suffering
    5. On the cross He paid for our sins

III. Conclusion
  A. *Can You Look at the Crucified and Believe?*
    1. Look at the cross and see a King?
    2. Look at His suffering and see the Savior?
  B. *Has the Lord Revealed His Plan of Redemption to*
    You?
  C. *Will You Accept This Rejected Savior Today?*

The Man of Sorrows

Series on the Cross   *Isaiah 53:3–4*

I. Introduction
    A. *Sorrow Is a Part of Life*
        1. Who has not known sorrow?
        2. Life begins with a cry and ends with a sigh
    B. *Christ Came to Bear Our Sorrows*
        1. He experienced sorrow
        2. He is able to comfort those who are sorrowing
    C. *Examining the Sorrows of Christ*

II. Body
    A. *The Sorrow of Rejection (v. 3)*
        1. "He is despised and rejected of men"
        2. Rejection brings the deepest of sorrows
            a. His love was rejected
            b. His truth was rejected
            c. His kingdom was rejected
        3. He was rejected by His people (John 1:11)
        4. He was rejected by those in His home area (Matt. 13:57–58)
        5. He was rejected by the religious leaders (Pharisees)
        6. He was rejected by the crowd at the cross (Matt. 27:39–43)
        7. Have you suffered the sorrow of rejection?
        8. Jesus knows how you feel . . . and cares
    B. *The Sorrow of Grief (v. 3)*
        1. All are acquainted with grief
            a. Tears are common to us all
            b. The grief of shattered dreams
            c. The grief of broken homes
            d. The grief that suffering by loved ones brings
            e. The grief of losing loved ones in death
        2. Our Lord was "acquainted with grief"
            a. He did not insulate Himself from grief
            b. His tears at the grave of Lazarus (John 11:30)
            c. His tears for Jerusalem (Luke 19:41–44)
        3. Christ enters into our grief

a. We can bring our deepest grief to Him
b. He waits at the throne of grace
c. He provides grace to help in the time of need (Heb. 4:16)
d. His grace is sufficient for our grief (2 Cor. 12:9)

C. *The Sorrow of Loneliness (v. 3)*
1. "We hid as it were our faces from him"
2. He walked that lonely road for you and me
    a. He prayed in Gethsemane alone (Luke 22:40–46)
    b. At His arrest, His disciples left Him alone (Matt. 26:56)
    c. He stood before the high priest alone (Luke 22:63–71)
    d. He was tried before Pilate alone (Luke 23)
    e. He was forsaken on the cross alone (Matt. 27:46)
3. He will never leave us alone
    a. "I am with you alway" (Matt. 28:20)
    b. "I will not leave you comfortless" (John 14:18)
    c. "I will never leave thee, nor forsake thee" (Heb. 13:5)

III. **Conclusion**
A. *Christ Has Carried Our Sorrows*
B. *Why Then Should We Carry Them?*
C. *Accept His Comfort for Your Sorrows*
D. *Share This Good News with Sorrowing Ones*

Wounds, Bruises, and Peace

Series on the Cross   *Isaiah 53:5*

I. Introduction
   A. *Perhaps the Most Moving Prophecy of the Cross*
      1. Here the price of redemption becomes personal
      2. Here is a preview of John 3:16
   B. *Details of Christ's Death on the Cross That Should Call Us to Faith*
      1. A text in which we can write our names
      2. All this suffering was for you and me
   C. *His Suffering Declares the Depths of His Love*

II. Body
   A. *Wounded for Me*
      1. "He was wounded for our transgressions"
      2. Who is this One who was wounded?
         a. One who was pierced (Zech. 12:10)
         b. One who wore a crown of thorns (Matt. 27:29)
         c. One who was nailed to the cross (John 20:25)
         d. One who was pierced by a soldier's spear (John 19:34)
      3. Why was He wounded?
         a. "For our transgressions"
         b. He had done nothing to deserve death (Luke 23:41)
         c. His wounds were because of His love for you and me
      4. Christ was our substitute
      5. The wounds of Christ were prophesied (Zech. 13:6)
      6. The wounds of Christ were in God's plan for our salvation
      7. The wounds of Christ were for me
   B. *Bruised for Me*
      1. "He was bruised for our iniquities"
      2. Imagine the bruises of the cross
         a. Bruises from the crown of thorns
         b. Bruises from the nails
         c. Bruises from the jolting of setting the cross

              d. Bruises from the writhing of His body against the cross

      3. Other thoughts about bruises

              a. Here was the bruising of the serpent's head (Gen. 3:15)

              b. He came to set those free who were bruised (Luke 4:18)

      4. Why was Christ bruised?

              a. For my transgressions

              b. How serious my sins!

              c. How wonderful His love!

  C. *Peace for Me*

      1. "The chastisement of our peace was upon him"

      2. There is a price for peace

      3. Our sins had separated us from God

      4. We were enemies of God (Rom. 5:10)

              a. This enmity was put away at the cross (Eph. 2:13–17)

              b. Peace was made for us at the cross (Col. 1:20)

      5. We have peace with God through faith in Christ (Rom. 5:1)

III. **Conclusion**

  A. *Wounds, Bruises, and Stripes*

      1. All these to make us whole

      2. Dead to sin and alive to righteousness (1 Peter 2:24)

  B. *His Suffering and Death for Our Peace*

      1. Have you stood alone at the cross?

      2. Have you seen Christ wounded, bruised, and beaten for you?

  C. *How Can You Delay Your Response to Calvary Love?*

Bringing Back the Strays

Series on the Cross   *Isaiah 53:6*

I. Introduction
   A. *A Text That Begins and Ends with "All"*
   B. *Great "Alls" of the Bible*
   1. "For all have sinned" (Rom. 3:23)
   2. "Who gave himself a ransom for all" (1 Tim. 2:6)
   3. "In him is no darkness at all" (1 John 1:5)
   4. "The blood of Jesus Christ his Son cleanseth us from all sin" (1 John 1:7)
   C. *How This Text Affects Us All*

II. Body
   A. *We Have All Gone Astray*
   1. "All we like sheep have gone astray"
   2. Eden's fall affects us all
      a. Not one person is righteous (Rom. 3:10)
      b. All have sinned and come short of God's glory (Rom. 3:23)
   3. Sin brought death (Gen. 3:3; Rom. 6:23)
      a. Spiritual death (Eph. 2:1)
      b. Physical death (Heb. 9:27)
   4. All creation has been affected by the fall (Rom. 8:22)
   5. Sin has placed us in deep trouble
      a. Apart from God's love there is no hope
      b. Thankfully, He loves us so there is hope (Rom. 5:8)
   B. *We Have All Gone Our Own Way*
   1. "We have turned every one to his own way"
   2. We have chosen to rebel against God
      a. Rebelling against His laws
      b. Rebelling against His love
      c. Rebelling against His goodness
      d. Rebelling against His grace
   3. Rebellion against Christ when He came to save
      a. "We will not have this man to reign over us" (Luke 19:14)
      b. This attitude led to the Cross

    4.   Rebellion continues today

       a.   Some will not receive Christ and be saved

       b.   Even some believers choose their own way

  C. *Christ Died Our Debt of Sin to Pay*

    1.   "The LORD hath laid on him the iniquity of us all"

    2.   Jesus paid it all

       a.   He voluntarily paid our debt of sin

       b.   He became the propitiation for our sins (1 John 4:10)

       c.   He became sin for us (2 Cor. 5:21)

       d.   We are redeemed by His blood (1 Peter 1:18–20)

    3.   Our redemption by His blood is the theme of heaven (Rev. 1:5)

       a.   It is heaven's song (Rev. 5:9)

       b.   It will be the joy of saints and angels (Rev. 7:9–17)

III. Conclusion

  A. *Do You Accept the Fact of Your Sinfulness?*

  B. *Do You Admit Your Rebellion Against God?*

  C. *Will You Accept the One Who Bore Your Sins at the Cross?*

The Silent Savior

Series on the Cross   *Isaiah 53:7*

I. Introduction
   A. *Isaiah Keeps Developing the Details of Redemption*
      1. The Man of sorrows, the despised One (v. 3)
      2. The smitten Redeemer carrying our sorrows (v. 4)
      3. The wounded One who brings us peace (v. 5)
      4. The One who carries the sins of the straying sheep (v. 6)
   B. *The Character of Christ*
      1. His discipline under oppression
      2. His control during the pressure of the cross
   C. *The Silence of Christ Proclaimed His Strength*

II. Body
   A. *Christ Was Silent When Oppressed*
      1. He was arrested though innocent (Matt. 26:47–56)
         a. Sold by Judas for thirty pieces of silver
         b. Betrayed with a kiss
      2. He was falsely accused but held His peace (Matt. 26:60–63)
      3. He was silent when His followers failed Him
         a. They forsook Him and fled (Matt. 26:56)
         b. Peter denied Him three times (Matt. 26:69–75)
      4. Peter's later description of the silent Savior (1 Peter 2:23)
         a. "When he was reviled, reviled not again"
         b. "When he suffered, he threatened not"
      5. He was silent before Pilate (Matt. 27:14)
      6. Compare His silence to ours when we are oppressed
   B. *Christ Was Silent When Afflicted*
      1. Silent when He was scourged (Matt. 27:26)
      2. Silent when mocked by the soldiers (Matt. 27:29–35)
         a. The crown of thorns and reed scepter
         b. Bowing before Him saying "Hail, King of the Jews"
         c. They spat on Him and struck Him
         d. Gambling for His garments

    3. Silent when mocked by the crowd (Matt. 27:39–44)
    4. Paul's description of His silence (Phil. 2:5–7)
        a. "He made himself of no reputation"
        b. "He humbled himself"
        c. "He became obedient unto death"
    5. What an example for us when we are afflicted!
  C. *Christ Was the Silent Lamb*
    1. "As a lamb to the slaughter"
    2. Isaiah looks back to the Passover lamb (Exod. 12)
        a. The lamb that brought deliverance from Egypt
        b. The lamb that brought freedom from oppression
        c. The lamb that rescued them from their afflictions
    3. Isaiah also looks forward to the Lamb of God
        a. The Lamb whose death would deliver those who believe
        b. The Lamb whose blood would cleanse us from our sins
    4. John the Baptist: "Behold the Lamb of God" (John 1:29)

III. **Conclusion**
  A. *Are You Moved by the Silence of the Lamb?*
  B. *Will You Come in Faith to the Oppressed and Afflicted One?*
  C. *The Silent Savior Invites You to Trust Him and Be Free*

From the Cross to the Throne

I. **Introduction**
  A. *Isaiah's Great Prophecy of the Cross*
     1. Every event leading to Calvary is in this chapter
     2. All the pain and suffering of the cross is here
        a. The rejection of the Redeemer
        b. The wounds of our Savior
        c. The suffering of the great Shepherd
        d. The silence of the Lamb slain for sinners
  B. *The Moving Account of Key Characters at the Crucifixion (vv. 8–9)*
     1. The soldiers and the crucifixion
     2. The wicked and the rich
        a. Crucified between two thieves
        b. Wealthy Joseph's grave provided for Him

II. **Body**
  A. *Resurrection (v. 10)*
     1. The cross was in God's plan
        a. It pleased the Lord to bruise Him
        b. This was no afterthought with God
     2. His soul became an offering for sin
        a. Consider all the offerings of the centuries
        b. These were types that foreshadowed the coming cross
     3. A prophecy of the resurrection
        a. "He shall prolong his days"
        b. The pleasure of the LORD: God's plan developing
     4. Here is the Gospel (1 Cor. 15:3–4)
     5. The Cross and resurrection are God's good news
  B. *Justification (v. 11)*
     1. Divine satisfaction
        a. The travail of the soul of Christ
        b. His suffering and death sufficient
        c. Sin's debt was paid at the cross
     2. God could be just and the justifier (Rom. 3:24–26)
     3. The cry from the cross: "It is finished" (John 19:30)

        a. Redemption was complete
        b. Justification for all who believe (Rom. 3:26)
        c. Justification by faith brings peace with God (Rom. 5:1)

C. *Intercession (v. 12)*
    1. From the cross to the kingdom
        a. "He made himself of no reputation" (Phil 2:7)
        b. Obedient to the death of the cross (Phil 2:8)
        c. God has exalted Him (Phil. 2:9)
        d. His name is above every name (Phil. 2:9)
        e. Every knee shall bow before Him (Phil. 2:10)
    2. Christ interceded for sinners on the cross
        a. He "made intercession for the transgressors"
        b. "Father, forgive them"
    3. The intercession of Christ today
        a. "Who also maketh intercession for us" (Rom. 8:34)
        b. "He ever liveth to make intercession" (Heb. 7:25)
        c. "We have an advocate with the Father" (1 John 2:1)

III. Conclusion
    A. *Christ Died: The Debt Is Paid*
    B. *Christ Is Risen: He Is Able to Save*
    C. *Christ Intercedes: He Represents Us Before the Throne*

Resurrection Power

Series on the Resurrection Begins   *Luke 24:1–12*

I. Introduction
 A. *A Day of Good News*
  1. The day of Christ's resurrection
  2. Without the resurrection there is no good news
 B. *Events of the Cross and After*
  1. The upper room promises to the disciples
  2. The betrayal by Judas and the trial before Pilate
  3. The crucifixion and the seven last words
  4. The despair of those who came to the tomb (v. 1)
 C. *Then Came the Resurrection*
 D. *What Power!*

II. Body
 A. *The Power of the Resurrection Is Almighty Power (vv. 2–3)*
  1. The stone was rolled away
  2. The body of Christ was gone
  3. This is the age of power
   a. Automobiles, planes, spacecraft
   b. The power of knowledge: scientific breakthroughs
   c. Nuclear power: domestic and destructive
  4. Resurrection power is the greatest of all
   a. The power to restore life
   b. What can science do in a cemetery?
  5. The power of the Trinity involved in the resurrection
   a. The Power of the Son (John 10:17–18)
   b. The power of the Father (Eph. 1:18–20)
   c. The Power of the Holy Spirit (Rom. 1:4)
 B. *The Power of the Resurrection Is Amazing Power (vv. 4–11)*
  1. Here is power to save the soul (Amazing Grace)
  2. No hope apart from the resurrection (1 Cor. 15:13–20)
  3. The power of Christ to save:
   a. His life: the perfection needed to save

   b. His death: the payment needed to save

   c. His resurrection: the power needed to save

  4. "Why seek ye the living among the dead?"

   a. We were all spiritually dead (Eph. 2:1)

   b. All can come to Christ and be made alive

   c. No case is too difficult for Him (Heb. 7:25)

   d. Come to Christ in faith and find life

 C. *The Power of the Resurrection Is Available Power (v. 12)*

  1. Power is worthless unless available

   a. Power plants must be wired to homes and factories

   b. Power must be transmitted to be of any use

  2. God has made resurrection power available to us

   a. Are you tempted? Claim resurrection power

   b. Are you depressed? Claim resurrection power

   c. Are you defeated? Claim resurrection power

  3. Do not put off salvation for fear you can't live the life

   a. Our living Lord will keep those He saves

   b. Resurrection power makes it possible

  4. Even defeated Peter found hope at the empty tomb

III. Conclusion

 A. *Trust the One with Resurrection Power to Save You*

 B. *Claim Resurrection Power to Live for Him*

Experiences at the Empty Tomb

Series on the Resurrection   *Matthew 28:1–10*

I. Introduction
   A. *The Supposed Victories at the Cross*
1. The priests: rid of the One who spoke with authority
2. The Pharisees: rid of the One who rebuked their hypocrisy
3. The politicians: rid of the one who caused this tumult

   B. *The Certain Victory of the Resurrection*
1. The promise of resurrection was fulfilled (John 2:19)
2. The deity of Christ was guaranteed (Rom. 1:4)
3. The empty tomb remains the greatest miracle of all time

   C. *What the Empty Tomb Meant to Those Who Were There*

II. Body
   A. *The Angel at the Empty Tomb (vv. 1–3)*
1. The women coming to do the work of undertakers
   a. They were sincere but doubted Christ's promise
   b. They expected He would be in the tomb
2. Earth shaking events greeted these women
   a. There was a great earthquake
   b. The angel of the Lord descended
   c. The angel rolled back the stone from the door
   d. The angel sat on the stone
3. Angels and the coming rapture (1 Thess. 4:13–18)
   a. The voice of the archangel
   b. The trump of God
   c. Empty graves and believers caught up
   d. The Lord knows the location of every grave
4. The angel sitting on the stone shows Christ conquered death

   B. *Anxiety at the Empty Tomb (vv. 4–5)*
1. Roman soldiers guarding the tomb (Matt. 27:62–66)

        a.   The priests and Pharisees feared Christ might rise

        b.   Pilate assigned a guard to secure the grave

    2.   The soldiers and the angel of the Lord

        a.   They began to tremble when they saw the angel

        b.   They fainted (became as dead men)

    3.   The soldiers had good reasons to shake

        a.   They would have to give an account to their superiors

        b.   They knew now that Christ was the Son of God

        c.   They had been wrong in their rejection of Him

    4.   Have you been rejecting Christ?

    5.   Someday you will be face-to-face with reality

    6.   Strangely, the women were also afraid

  C.   *The Assurance Given at the Empty Tomb (vv. 5–10)*

    1.   No word of assurance given to the soldiers

    2.   Faith builders for frightened women

        a.   "Fear not"—What good words in trembling times!

        b.   "For I know"—God knows all about us

        c.   "He is not here"—Good news!

        d.   "He is risen"—Hallelujah!

        e.   "As he said"—God keeps His word

        f.   "Go quickly and tell"—Missionaries for Christ

        g.   "He goeth before you"—(John 10:4)

III. Conclusion

  A.   *What Does the Empty Tomb Mean to Us?*

  B.   *The Empty Tomb Should Move Us to Spiritual Reality*

  C.   *The Empty Tomb Should Assure Us That Christ Is Alive Today*

If Christ Had Not Risen

Series on the Resurrection   *1 Corinthians 15:13–20*

I. **Introduction**
  A. *Promises of the Resurrection*
    1. Raising the temple in three days (John 2:18–22)
    2. The sign of Jonah (Matt. 12:40)
    3. Jesus prophesies His resurrection (Mark 8:31)
  B. *Millions Worldwide Celebrate the Resurrection*
  C. *But What If Christ Had Not Risen?*

II. **Body**
  A. *All Preaching Would Be Vain (v. 14)*
    1. Every sermon delivered would be worthless
      a. All sermon preparation futile
      b. All preaching a waste of energy
      c. All listening to sermons a waste of time
    2. All the preaching of the past would have no value
      a. The preaching of the apostles
      b. The preaching of early church martyrs
      c. The preaching of giants of the faith
        (1) Luther's sermons that brought the reformation
        (2) Wesley's sermons that brought revival to England
        (3) Moody's sermons that brought thousands to Christ
    3. If Christ has not risen, we shouldn't be here
  B. *All Faith Would Be Vain (v. 14)*
    1. Faith . . . that saves the soul (Acts 16:31)
      a. That brings peace with God (Rom. 5:1)
      b. That accepts the gift of grace (Eph. 2:8–9)
    2. Faith . . . that makes prayer powerful
      a. "If thou canst believe" (Mark 9:23)
      b. "Great and mighty things" (Jer. 33:3)
    3. Faith . . . that brings peace of mind
      a. "Be careful for nothing" (Phil. 4:6–8)
      b. "Whom shall I fear?" (Ps. 27:1)
  C. *All Hope of Heaven Would Be Gone (v. 18)*
    1. The dead in Christ would have perished

      2. Every grave would be a place of despair
         a. No mansions prepared for us (John 14:1–3)
         b. No better place waiting (Phil. 1:23)
         c. No hope of meeting departed loved ones
            (1 Thess. 4:13)
      3. Promises of heaven would be false

    D. *All Believers Would Be Miserable (v. 19)*
      1. We would have believed a lie
      2. We would have spent our lives following a fable
      3. The joy we profess would have been a deception
      4. We would have traded earthly gain for a dream

III. Conclusion
    A. *But Christ Is Risen! (vv. 20–26)*
      1. Gospel preaching is powerful and true
      2. Faith in Christ brings forgiveness and eternal life
      3. Believers go to heaven when they die
      4. Christians have reasons to rejoice
    B. *We Will Rise to Be Like Him (v. 20)*
    C. *Christ Will Reign Forever (vv. 25–26)*
    D. *Does Christ Reign in Your Heart?*

Many Infallible Proofs

I. **Introduction**
   A. *Christ Is Risen!*
      1. He had promised His resurrection
      2. The Bible declares His resurrection
      3. We believe in His resurrection
   B. *Some Doubt the Resurrection*
      1. They demand proof of the resurrection
      2. The Bible says there are many infallible proofs
   C. *Consider the Proofs of the Resurrection*

II. **Body**
   A. *The Empty Tomb*
      1. The enemies of Christ remembered His promise of resurrection
         a. They told Pilate of this promise (Matt. 26:63)
         b. They secured soldiers to guard the tomb (v. 65)
         c. The tomb was officially sealed (v. 66)
      2. The friends of Jesus forgot His promise of resurrection
         a. Women came to the tomb to anoint His body
         b. Strange, His enemies remembered and His friends forgot
         c. Matthew Henry: "Hate is keener sighted than love"
      3. When the women arrived the tomb was empty (Matt. 28:1–8)
      4. Even the soldiers admitted the tomb was empty (28:11)
      5. The enemies of Christ knew the tomb was empty (28:12–15)
         a. They held a meeting to decide how to deal with it
         b. They bribed the soldiers to tell an unbelievable lie
         c. Their precautions and panic prove the resurrection
         d. Their lie continues to this day

67

B. *The Eyewitnesses*
    1. Eyewitness testimony holds up in court
    2. Who were these eyewitnesses?
        a. The women who came to the tomb
            (Luke 23:55–24:11)
        b. Peter and John (John 20:1–10)
        c. The Emmaus Disciples (Luke 24:13–35)
        d. Thomas, after one weak week (John 20:24–29)
        e. More than five hundred others (1 Cor. 15:6)
        f. James and all of the apostles (15:7)
        g. Paul on the road to Damascus (15:8)
    3. Why would anyone doubt these honest people?
C. *The Energizing of the Disciples*
    1. The disciples had been devastated by the
        crucifixion
        a. They had forsaken Christ and fled (Matt.
            26:56)
        b. Some were going home (Luke 24:13–35)
    2. The resurrection changed everything
        a. Fear was changed to faith
        b. Doubters were changed to dynamic witnesses
    3. These former cowards became courageous
        a. They laid their lives on the line
        b. People do not die for a lie
        c. Thousands saved because of their witness
        d. The church exists because of this change

III. Conclusion

A. *The Greatest Proof Is the Change Christ Makes in
    Lives Today*
B. *He Wants to Change You (2 Cor. 5:17)*
C. *Meet the Living Christ by Faith (Rom. 10:9–13)*
D. *You Will Be Another Infallible Proof of the Resurrection*

God Questions Earth's First Killer

Genesis 4:6

I. Introduction
A. *The First Family*
1. Adam and Eve had been told to have children (Gen. 1:28)
2. This command given before the fall
3. Proves sex in marriage has always been right (Heb. 13:4)
4. Cain and Abel and other children born (4:1–2; 5:4)
B. *A Violent Attitude Enters the First Family*
1. Abel a shepherd and man of faith (Heb. 11:4)
2. Cain a farmer and not right with God
   a. He was jealous of Abel
   b. He hated his brother
   c. He was controlled by anger
C. *God's Questions to an Angry Man*

II. Body
A. *These Are Questions That Show God's Interest in Our Feelings*
1. Why are you angry?
2. Why are you feeling down?
3. Do these questions from God apply to you today?
   a. Are you angry?
   b. Are you depressed?
   c. Are you jealous of another person's gain?
   d. Is hate beginning to grow in your heart?
   e. Is your bad attitude showing in your face?
4. When Elijah cried out, God cared (1 Kings 19)
5. When Jonah pouted outside of Ninevah, God cared (Jonah 4)
6. God cares about your troubled heart
B. *These Are Questions That Reveal the Cause of the First Murder*
1. Every act starts as a thought
2. John wrote about Cain's downfall (1 John 3:10–16)
   a. His works were evil
   b. He was convicted by the righteousness of Abel

   c. He didn't love his brother
   d. His hate determined his fate—"Whosoever hateth his brother is a murderer" (v. 15)
  3. What destructive thoughts are you entertaining?
   a. Lustful thoughts that may lead to sexual sin?
   b. Covetous thoughts that may lead to dishonesty?
   c. Hateful thoughts that may lead to violence, even murder?
 C. *These Are Questions Intended to Change Cain's Life*
  1. God acts out of His love
  2. Loving instruction followed these questions
   a. God tells Cain how to be accepted by Him
   b. God warns Cain of the danger of continuing in sin
  3. God meets us where we are
  4. God wants us to change course (repent)
  5. God calls us to look to Him in faith

III. Conclusion
 A. *What Might Have Been*
  1. Cain could have forsaken his anger and unbelief
  2. Cain could have responded to God's love
 B. *So Can You!*
 C. *Let God Replace Your Bitterness with His Blessings*

You Must Be Born Again

John 3:1–21

I. Introduction

A. *New Life for a Religious Man*
1. Many have religion but not spiritual reality
2. Many have a form of godliness but not faith
3. In this text a religious man learns about new life

B. *Why Wesley Preached Often on Being Born Again*
1. His answer: "Because you must be born again"
2. Have you been born again?

C. *The Man Who Learned About Being Born Again*

II. Body

A. *Nicodemas and His Need (vv. 1–2)*
1. Nicodemas came to Jesus at night
    a. He was a ruler of the Jews
    b. Probably afraid others would see him
    c. Afraid he might lose credibility with his friends
2. Why Nicodemas came to Jesus
    a. He had heard of His miracles
    b. He believed God was with him
3. What Nicodemas did not need
    a. He did not need religion; he was a Pharisee
    b. He did not need acclaim; he was a ruler of the Jews
4. He didn't recognize his real need until he was with Jesus
5. He needed to be born again

B. *The Savior and His Strange Statement (vv. 3–7)*
1. Jesus was available even at night
    a. He was never too tired or busy for people
    b. Jesus always has time for those who come to Him
2. Jesus went past the words of Nicodemas to his real problem
    a. He knows why you are here today
    b. He understands the problems that trouble you
    c. He knows about your upset home; your dread of death

    3. "Except a man be born again"
      a. No other way to enter the kingdom of God
      b. No other way to be sure of heaven
    4. "How can a man be born when he is old?"
      a. Nicodemas is confused by the strange statement
      b. He thinks Jesus is talking about another physical birth

C. *Christ Makes It Clear (vv. 3–16)*
    1. Answering the questions of a religious man
      a. This is not another physical birth
      b. "That which is born of the flesh is flesh"
      c. "This is a spiritual birth"
      d. "That which is born of the Spirit is spirit"
    2. "How can these things be?"
    3. Clearing up the confusion
      a. Moses and the serpent in the wilderness (v. 14)
      b. Israelites who looked in faith lived (Num. 21:9)
      c. Those who look to Christ in faith receive eternal life
    4. The clearest verse of all (v. 16)

III. Conclusion

A. *Summarizing the New Birth*
    1. It is the work of the Holy Spirit (Titus 3:5)
    2. It the result of faith in Christ (John 3:14–16)

B. *Have You Been Born Again?*

Paul's Crown of Rejoicing

1 Thessalonians 2:19–20

I. Introduction
A. *Paul's Double Anticipation*
1. His meeting with Christ at his return
2. His meeting then with those he had won to Christ
B. *What Converts Meant to Paul*
1. They were his hope and joy (v. 19)
2. They were his crown of rejoicing (v. 19)
3. They were his glory and joy (v. 20)
C. *What His Love for Souls Did for Paul's Life*

II. Body
A. *The Desire of Paul's Heart (Rom. 10:1)*
1. His heart's desire was for Israel to be saved
a. This was his constant prayer
b. It was priority one on his prayer list
2. What is the desire of your heart?
a. A new home, a better job, a new car?
b. How do these compare with desiring souls to be saved?
3. When Paul was hungry, he desired souls more than food
4. When Paul was thirsty, he desired souls more than water
5. When Paul was in jail, he desired souls more than freedom
6. When before judges, he desired souls more than justice
B. *The Deciding Factor in Paul's Behavior (1 Cor. 9:19–22)*
1. He used every means to save some
a. He served others to win them to Christ (v. 19)
b. He spoke to Jews as a Jew to win them (v. 20)
c. He met people where they were to win them (v. 21)
d. He appeared weak to the weak that He might win them
2. In prison, Paul praised God to win souls (Acts 16:25–32)

73

   3. After being stoned, Paul rose and kept preaching to
       win souls
   4. What's different about your behavior?
       a. Is this because of your concern for souls?
       b. Is it only to impress others?
       c. Are you careful not to cause others to stumble?
       d. How is your life affected because of a concern
           for souls?

C. *The Desperation in Paul's Manner and Message*
    (2 Cor. 6:1–2)
    1. Paul's manner and message were driven by his
        concern for souls
    2. Note his urgency:
        a. Now is the accepted time
        b. Now is the day of salvation
    3. Each day was a day of harvest and urgency to Paul
    4. Paul warned against procrastination
        a. King Agrippa: "Almost thou persuadest me"
        b. Felix: "A more convenient season"
        c. Many postpone salvation and are lost

III. **Conclusion**
    A. *The Result: Many Souls Won in Paul's Ministry*
    B. *The Crown of Glory*
        1. Who will you meet on heaven's street?
        2. Who will be there because you cared?
        3. What is the most important thing in your life?
        4. Are you looking forward to meeting those you've
            won?
    C. *Are You Ready for the Day of Christs Return?*
    D. *Will You Receive the Crown of Rejoicing?*

Hindrances to Faith

Galatians 5:7

I. Introduction
   A. *Four Sad Words: "You Did Run Well"*
      1. They speak of past blessings
      2. They speak of present failure
   B. *What Were Some Former Blessings in Galatia?*
      1. Their first contact with the Gospel (4:13)
      2. Their reception and care of Paul (4:14)
      3. Their love for Paul (4:15)
      4. Their former obedience to the truth (3:1)
   C. *Hindrances That Caused Their Decline*

II. Body
   A. *The Hindrance of False Teachers (1:1–9)*
      1. Paul's tender greeting
         a. Confirming his calling (v. 1)
         b. Grace and peace sent to these believers (v. 3)
         c. Rehearsing the Gospel (v. 4)
         d. To God be the glory (v. 5)
      2. False teachers had come to confuse the Galatians
         a. Not really concerned with reaching the lost
         b. Preying on those already trusting in Christ
         c. This is so true today
      3. Strong language condemning false teachers
         a. Some are perverting the Gospel (v. 7)
         b. Let those who do so be accursed (v. 8)
      4. The nature of the false teaching
         a. A mixture of law and grace for salvation
         b. Lawkeeping taught for believers
      5. Refuting this false teaching (Gal. 2:15–21; 3:1–9)
   B. *The Hindrance of Fighting Christians (5:15)*
      1. Biting and devouring one another
      2. Believers are to show love, not hate
         a. The proof of discipleship (John 13:35)
         b. "Love thy neighbor as thyself" (v. 14)
      3. This was the problem in Corinth (1 Cor. 3:1–4)
         a. Strife and divisions marks of carnality
         b. Following men instead of Christ
      4. Bitterness and strife are from Satan (James 3:14–16)

     5.   Peace among believers is from the Lord (James 3:17–18)

C. *The Hindrance of Those Given to the Works of the Flesh (vv. 17–21)*

     1.   Contrasting the works of the flesh and the Spirit
         a.   The battle: the flesh and the Spirit
         b.   The victory: "Walk in the Spirit"
     2.   Surrounded by the works of the flesh
         a.   Plots for most entertainment
         b.   Headlines for daily newspapers
     3.   Believers must not be overcome by the flesh
     4.   The fruit of the Spirit is to flow through us (5:22–23)
         a.   The joy of the Spirit-filled life
         b.   The fruit of the Spirit honors our Lord

III. Conclusion

A. *Did You Once Serve Christ Better Than Today*

B. *Who Has Hindered You?*

C. *Return to the Place of Full Surrender to Him*

Reasons to Praise the Lord

1 Peter 1:1–7

I. Introduction
A. *A Letter from Peter*
1. A man who had trouble with his temper
2. A man who had trouble with temptation
3. A man who had trouble with his tongue
4. To know Peter well is to know ourselves well

B. *A Letter to Believers (v. 2)*

C. *A Letter That Begins with Reasons to Praise the Lord*

II. Body
A. *God Has Given Us a Living Hope (v. 3)*
1. "Unto a lively hope"
2. The condition of all people without Christ
   a. They have no real hope (Eph. 2:12)
   b. They may have false hope (Prov. 11:7)
3. Contrast these to Peter's living hope
   a. Christ is alive (Rom 1:4)
   b. Our salvation is guaranteed (1 Cor. 15:3–6)
   c. Our similar resurrection is sure (1 Cor. 15:20–23)

B. *God Has Given Us a Lasting Inheritance (v. 4)*
1. Peter was the son of a poor fisherman
2. His earthly inheritance would have been small
3. He had left all to follow Christ
   a. Even left his small inheritance
   b. Friends and relatives may have wondered
   c. What's wrong with Peter?
   d. Doesn't he have any thought for his future?
4. Now Peter realizes he has a great inheritance ahead
   a. One that is incorruptible; won't decay
   b. One that is undefiled; pure
   c. One that will not fade away; not a mirage
   d. One that is reserved in heaven
5. We are perishing people among perishing things
6. In Christ, we do not perish, nor does our inheritance

C. *God Has Given Us a Lifetime of Powerful Protection (v. 5–7)*
1. "Who are kept by the power of God"

        a.   "Kept" here is military word
        b.   We are guarded by the power of God
   2.   Our Lord cares for us every day
   3.   He provides power to overcome temptation
   4.   Even our testings and trials are temporary (v. 6)
        a.   The trying of our faith more precious than gold
        b.   Problems now . . . praise later, at the Lord's
           return

III.   **Conclusion**
   A.   *Peter Blesses the Lord*
      1.   In view of his living hope
      2.   In view of his lasting inheritance
      3.   In view of his lifetime of powerful protection
   B.   *Good Reasons for Us to Also Praise the Lord*
   C.   *Praise the Lord!*

Caleb's Charge

I. Introduction
    A. *A Special Time for the Children of Israel*
        1. They had been delivered from slavery
        2. They had been set free by the blood of the Passover Lamb
        3. They had been protected and provided for on their journey
        4. They had reached the edge of the Promised Land
    B. *The Spies and Their Reports (vv. 26–29)*
        1. Moses had sent twelve spies to scout the land
        2. They all brought back a good report of the land
        3. Ten spies feared the people who lived there
    C. *Caleb Charged His People to Move Forward*

II. Body
    A. *A Charge to Expect Harmony among God's People*
        1. He stilled the people before Moses
        2. "Let us go up at once"
            a. He sees the people moving as one
            b. He expects no hesitation (at once)
        3. God's people are powerful when they move together
        4. Biblical examples of harmony among God's people
            a. How good and how pleasant (Ps. 133)
            b. The early church and its power (Acts 1:14; 2:1)
        5. Most churches decline because of strife (1 Cor. 3)
        6. Let's expect God to heal wounds and bring us together
    B. *A Charge to Expect the Hand of God among His People*
        1. "And possess it"
        2. "We are well able to overcome it"
        3. This could not happen in their own strength
        4. We are unstoppable in the power of God
            a. Waiting on Him we renew our strength (Isa. 40:31)
            b. "I can do all things through Christ" (Phil. 4:13)

  5. Caleb sees the people moving ahead in God's power

    a. Why not the same vision for our church?

    b. Enough of this timid, faithless approach

    c. Let's believe God and move ahead

 C. *A Charge to Share in the Harvest Intended for God's People*

  1. The sample brought back by the spies (vv. 23–24)

  2. Caleb longed for another taste of the fruit of Canaan

  3. We need to get involved in the harvest

    a. When we do, our problems are put away

    b. Our focus is off ourselves and on others

  4. The harvest is ready (John 4:35)

  5. The wages for reaping are great (John 4:36)

  6. The laborers are few (Matt. 9:37)

  7. One of life's greatest opportunities

III. Conclusion

 A. *Why Caleb Could Make Such a Powerful Charge*

  1. Others saw the giants; Caleb saw the Lord

  2. Others saw big giants and a little God

  3. Caleb saw a big God and little giants

 B. *Let's Accept Caleb's Charge*

  1. A harvest of souls awaits

  2. We can reap and claim new territory together

The Mother of Us All

Genesis 4

I. Introduction
   A. *Mother's Day and Motherhood*
      1. Families are part of God's plan
      2. God ordained the home, not the herd
   B. *Eve, the Mother of All Living (Gen. 3:20)*
      1. Lessons from the first mother
      2. Eve's hope, her heartache, her highest happiness

II. Body
   A. *A Mother's Hope (v. 1)*
      1. "I have gotten a man from the Lord"
      2. Understanding Eve's statement requires background of it
      3. The creation of Adam and Eve (1:26–27; 2:18–25)
         a. Adam was created first . . . from the dust
         b. Eve created from Adam's rib
            (1) The first anesthesia and surgery
            (2) From Adam's side; next to his heart
      4. The first marriage
         a. God joined Adam and Eve to be one for life
         b. Bone of my bone and flesh of my flesh (2:23)
         c. A picture of Christ and the church
      5. The temptation, the fall, and the promised seed (3:15)
      6. Eve thought Cain was the promised man to bruise the serpent
      7. Christ would finally come and fulfill that promise
   B. *A Mother's Heartache (v. 8)*
      1. Birth was an entirely new experience
      2. The joy of that little boy being born
         a. His first words and steps
         b. The blessings of motherhood
      3. Abel and daughters soon followed
         a. A happy home full of love
         b. Cain became a farmer; Abel a keeper of sheep
      4. Then came that heartbreaking day: Cain killed Abel

  5. We don't know how Cain killed Abel
      a. If a knife, it entered also into Eve's heart
      b. If a club, it battered Eve
      c. Our sins always affect those we love
  6. Mothers have wept rivers of tears over wayward
      children
C. *A Mother's Highest Happiness (vv. 25–26)*
  1. Could Eve forget Cain's violence?
  2. Could Eve forget Abel's death?
  3. No, but she could recover
      a. God brings recovering love
      b. His grace is always sufficient
  4. Seth was born as a substitute for Abel
  5. Christ became our substitute on the cross
  6. Seth brought Eve great joy
      a. Seth's son, Enoch, brought revival
      b. "Then began men to call upon the name of the
          Lord"

III. Conclusion
A. *God Meets Us Where We Are*
  1. He met Eve in her grief over Cain and Abel
  2. He will meet you in your time of trouble
B. *God Meets Troubled Mothers and Encourages Them*
C. *God Meets Wayward Children and Calls Them to
      Himself*

Mary, Martha, and the Master

Luke 10:38–42

I. **Introduction**
   A. *The Journeys of Jesus*
      1. Frequently took Him to Bethany
      2. To the home of Mary, Martha and Lazarus
      3. A place where Jesus felt at home
      4. Does Jesus feel at home in your house?
   B. *The Experience in Bethany That Describes Us All*
      1. Mary sitting at the feet of Jesus
      2. Martha laboring and complaining

II. **Body**
   A. *Mary Listening (v. 39)*
      1. "Mary sat at Jesus' feet, and heard his word"
         a. The place of submission (Luke 8:41)
         b. The place of devotion (John 12:3)
         c. The place of peace (Luke 8:35)
      2. Mary is an example of a Christian learning
      3. Mary is an example of a Christian worshiping
      4. Mary is an example of a Christian having devotions
      5. We must learn to sit at Jesus' feet and listen
         a. Without this we will not grow
         b. Without this we will be overcome by temptation
         c. Without this we will become carnal
   B. *Martha Laboring (v. 40)*
      1. "Martha was cumbered about much serving"
      2. Beware of the barrenness of busy-ness
      3. We must not be harsh with Martha
         a. There was work to be done
         b. Jesus and His disciples must be fed
         c. Other responsibilities may have been pressing
      4. See what work without worship did to Martha
         a. It caused her to be upset
         b. It caused her to talk instead of listen
         c. It caused her to be critical of her sister
         d. It caused her to doubt the love of Christ
         e. It caused her to be discouraged

  C. *The Master's Love (vv. 41–42)*
    1. "Martha, Martha" compared to other tender texts:
      a. "Simon, Simon," when attacked by Satan (Luke 22:31)
      b. "Saul, Saul," on the road to Damascus (Acts 9:4)
    2. "Thou art careful and troubled"
      a. Christ looks within and sees the troubled heart
      b. He knows all about our cares
      c. We are to cast our cares on Him (1 Peter 5:7)
    3. Martha's important omission
      a. Worship is the one thing needful
      b. Too often we leave out the most important thing
      c. Labor must be balanced by listening to Jesus

III. **Conclusion**
  A. *Mary's Lasting Reward (v. 42)*
    1. "Mary hath chosen that good part"
    2. This would never be taken away from her
  B. *What Is Most Needful in Your Life?*
  C. *You Will Find It Listening at Jesus' Feet*

Do What You Can

I. Introduction

A. *Our Lord at the House of a Leper (vv. 1–3)*
   1. Those were days of danger
      a. The Passover plot to destroy Jesus
      b. The priests and scribes restrained by the people
   2. Jesus entertained at the house of Simon the Leper
   3. How like our Lord to be with the outcasts of society

B. *The Woman and Her Precious Ointment*
   1. Giving what we have to Jesus brings blessing
   2. Giving all to Jesus also brings criticism (vv. 4–5)

C. *The Woman Commended: "She Hath Done What She Could"*
   1. A good example for all
   2. What you can do

II. Body

A. *Do What You Can to Build Up Your Faith (1 John 5:4)*
   1. We overcome through faith
   2. We are as effective as our faith enables us to be
   3. Take time to develop strong faith
      a. Take time to read the Bible daily (Rom. 10:17)
      b. Take time to pray (Mark 11:22–24)
      c. Take time to be alone with God (Mark 14:32–41)
   4. Exercise your gifts by becoming active in your church
   5. Exercise your faith and it will grow
   6. Expect God to come through for you

B. *Do What You Can to Build Up Other Believers (Rom. 14:19)*
   1. We are all to edify (build up) one another
   2. Don't focus on the faults of other believers
      a. Never speak negatively of them
      b. Look for the best in them
      c. Christians aren't perfect . . . just forgiven
   3. Don't cause another to stumble (14:21)

a.   Consider weaker members of God's family
b.   Let concern for these govern your conduct
4.   When others are overcome, restore them (Gal. 6:1)
5.   Bear one another's burdens (Gal. 6:2)
6.   Be an example to other believers (1 Tim. 4:12)
a.   An example in word, in conversation, in love
b.   An example in spirit, in faith, in purity
C.   *Do What You Can to Build Up the Body of Christ (Eph. 4:11–16)*
1.   Building up the body through teaching
a.   Are you gifted to teach?
b.   Are you using that gift in the church?
2.   Building up the body through love
a.   Speaking in love
b.   Giving in love
c.   Encouraging in love
3.   Building up the body through evangelism
a.   "Making increase of the body"
b.   Sharing the Gospel every day

III.   Conclusion

A.   *Let's Do What We Can for Christ*
B.   *We Can Make a Difference in the Church and the World*
C.   *His "Well Done" Will Make Every Effort Worth It All*

The Banished Brought Home

2 Samuel 14:14

I. Introduction
  A. *David's Son, Absalom, Has Been Banished*
   1. The story begins with sin (13:1–18)
      a. Amnon, David's son, takes advantage of his sister, Tamar
      b. Two years later, Absalom kills Amnon (13:21–39)
   2. Three years of banishment for Absalom have passed
   3. David secretly longs for reconciliation with Absalom
  B. *Joab the Peacemaker (14:1–13)*
   1. Joab enlists a wise woman from Tekoah to help him
   2. This wise woman approaches David with a tale of her own
      a. One of her sons had killed the other
      b. She wants to forgive and restore the offender
      c. David is sympathetic to her situation and offers help
      d. She helps David see that he needs to forgive

II. Body
  A. *God's Banished Ones (v. 14)*
   1. The words of a wise woman
      a. Phillipson: "This is one of the noblest and profoundest declarations of Scripture"
      b. Her words declare God's grace to us all
   2. "We must needs die" (Rom. 6:23; Heb. 9:27)
   3. "We are as water spilt on the ground"
   4. We all suffer the effects of sin
      a. Looks back to the banishment from the Garden
      b. We are all God's banished ones (Rom. 5:12)
   5. Not one more sin is needed to be lost forever (John 3:17)
  B. *God Has Devised Means for His Banished to Be Returned (v. 14)*

1. God is no respecter of persons
   a. Peter agreed (Acts 10:34)
   b. Salvation is available to all (Rom. 10:13)
2. God has devised means for His banished to be returned
3. James M. Gray: "Let not the beautiful words of verse 14 escape you. How they suggest the love of God for us in Jesus Christ! He was the means devised that we might not be banished from His presence."
4. Jesus came to seek and save the lost (Luke 19:10)
5. The death of Christ on the cross the means of our salvation
   a. Christ died the "just for the unjust" (1 Peter 3:18)
   b. The goal: that He might bring us to God (3:18)

C. *The Banished Brought Home to Full Fellowship (v. 14)*
1. King David heeded the words of the wise woman
   a. He perceived that Joab had set him up (v. 19)
   b. He ordered Joab to bring Absalom home (v. 21)
2. Absalom was brought back to Jerusalem (v. 23)
   a. He was brought to his own house (v. 24)
   b. Didn't see David's face for two years (v. 24)
3. Our Lord's grace is greater than that of David
   a. We are brought into full fellowship upon salvation
   b. No waiting to be saved . . . now is the time (2 Cor. 6:1–2)

III. Conclusion
A. *The Banished Brought Home to Stay*
1. Upon receiving Christ we are part of God's family (John 1:12)
2. We have everlasting life (John 5:24)
B. *Respond to God's Call to Come Home Right Now*

A Call to Remember

I. **Introduction**

A. *Memorial Day: a Day for Remembering*
1. Set aside to remember those fallen in battle
2. We also remember all loved ones who have died

B. *The Bible and Remembering*
1. Joshua set up stones to remember crossing Jordan (Josh. 4:9)
2. Jesus told His disciples to remember His words (John 15:20)
3. In communion, we remember Christ's death for us (1 Cor. 11:23)

C. *God's People Were Commanded to Remember*

II. **Body**

A. *Remember the Leading of the Lord (vv. 1–2)*
1. "Remember all the way which the LORD thy God led thee"
2. Israel had stood here before and doubted
   a. This led to forty years of wandering
   b. Forty years of humbling
   c. Forty years of learning God leads His people
   d. Forty years of learning God's word is true
3. America has come through many difficult times
   a. Times when freedom's future has been unsure
   b. Times when basic freedoms have been under attack
   c. Times when foreign enemies have threatened
   d. Times when domestic problems seemed too serious to solve
4. God has led the nation through dark times
   a. We have triumphed over our enemies
   b. Times of refreshing have come from the Lord
   c. We need a spiritual refreshing (revival) again

B. *Remember the Chastening of the Lord (vv. 5–6)*
1. "Thou shalt also consider [remember]"
   a. A man chastens his children
   b. God sometimes chastens nations

89

    2. God chastened Israel

       a. Their doubts cost them forty years of wandering

       b. A generation missed out on the Promised Land

    3. God still chastens those He loves (Heb. 12:6)

       a. Why should Christians remember this?

       b. Is it important that Americans remember this?

    4. What is happening in America that might bring chastening?

       a. What about the abortion tragedy?

       b. What about the drug and alcohol tragedies?

       c. What about the moral catastrophe?

    5. A call to remember and repent before chastening falls

  C. *Remember the Faithfulness of the Lord (vv. 7–20)*

    1. "Remember the LORD thy God" (v. 18)

       a. He gives you power to get wealth

       b. He establishes His covenants

    2. How the Lord had been faithful to Israel

       a. Manna for food (v. 3)

       b. Clothing and health (v. 4)

    3. How God has been faithful to America

       a. Bountiful harvests, unimagined wealth

       b. Protection in battles; the blessings of freedom

III. Conclusion

  A. *A Call to Remember and Be Thankful*

  B. *A Call to Remember, Repent, and Return to the Lord*

A Famine in America?

Amos 8:11

I. Introduction

A. *Famine Is Almost Unknown in America*
   1. We have been blessed beyond description
   2. We have been the envy of the world
   3. Conditions can change
      a. Consider the seven years of famine in Egypt
      b. Only Joseph (a man of God) saved that nation

B. *The Famine of This Text Is Different*
   1. This is a famine for the Word of God
   2. We are accustomed to an abundance here also
   3. Still, famine could come through indifference
      a. There are signs of such indifference
      b. Few churches growing through evangelism
      c. Not many Christians take God's Word into their world

C. *What Would It Mean to Have a Famine for the Word of God*

II. Body

A. *A Nation without the Bible Is without Freedom (John 8:32)*
   1. "The truth shall make you free"
   2. "It is impossible to enslave a Bible reading people" —Horace Greely
   3. No wonder tyrants hate the Bible
   4. History reveals the Bible brings freedom
      a. The history of the founding of America
      b. The development of a nation based on the Bible
      c. God's preservation of the nation even in war
      d. Churches have been guardians of freedom
   5. Solid Bible preaching keeps us alert to freedom's value
   6. Bible reading people keep freedom alive in daily life

B. *A Nation without the Bible Is without Foundations (Matt. 7:24–29)*

91

    1. The life or land built on the Bible stands
       a. God's Word provides a solid foundation
       b. Building on the Bible we withstand life's storms
    2. Apart from the Bible there are no absolutes
       a. Everything becomes relative
       b. No one knows what's right and wrong
    3. The Bible provides a moral compass
       a. A moral compass for individuals
       b. A moral compass for the nation
    4. We must get back to the Bible
       a. To neglect the Bible is to starve the soul
       b. Results are the same as being in a famine

C. *A Nation Without the Bible Is Without Faith (Rom. 10:17)*
    1. Paul describes this problem in his own nation (Rom. 10:1–4)
       a. A zeal of God, but not according to knowledge
       b. They were ignorant of God's righteousness
    2. The Bible imparts seeds of faith
       a. Faith comes by hearing and hearing by the Word of God
       b. Born again of incorruptible seed (1 Peter 1:23)
    3. Neglecting the Bible is like having a famine for God's Word
    4. Great national wealth is found in the faith of its people

III. Conclusion

A. *Are You Hungry for the Word of God?*
B. *Devour It While It Is Available*
C. *Share the Scriptures and Prevent a National Famine*

What God Wants to Do in Your Life

Philippians 1:6

I. Introduction

A. *What Do You Want to Do with Your Life?*
   1. Most have hopes and dreams
   2. Some have plans and schemes
   3. Some have selfish desires and some long to help others

B. *What Does God Want to Do in Your Life?*
   1. A more important question
   2. One that has both temporal and eternal dimensions
   3. What is the answer to this question?

II. Body

A. *God Wants to Begin a Work in Your Life*
   1. "He which hath *begun*"
      a. This is surprising but true
      b. God wants to work in the lives of sinners
      c. Here is amazing grace ready to work in us
   2. This is the opposite of what we naturally want
      a. We want to reach for the stars
      b. We want to achieve financial success
      c. We want to climb higher
   3. God wants to reach down
      a. To meet and change a sinner
      b. To seal an individual as His own
   4. God invites you to become His child by faith (John 1:12)
   5. He wants to start His work of reconstruction in you today

B. *God Wants to Begin a Good Work in Your Life*
   1. "He which hath begun a GOOD work in you"
   2. God's work in us may not seem good at the beginning
      a. Begins with making us aware of our sins (Rom. 3:10–23)
      b. We learn that our good works are worthless (Isa. 64:6)
      c. We learn that we have earned only death (Rom. 6:23)

    3. Grace brings us hope
       a. God loves us; Christ died for us
       b. We move from conviction to conversion
    4. Faith in Christ brings many good things to us
       a. Forgiveness of sins
       b. Justification
       c. Assurance of heaven
       d. The indwelling of the Holy Spirit
       e. A purpose to live: the glory of God

C. *God Wants to Perform a Permanent Work in Your Life*
    1. "Will perform it until the day of Jesus Christ"
    2. Paul was "confident" this good work would last
    3. Summarizing God's good work in believers:
       a. God begins His work (v. 6)
       b. God continues His work (2:13)
       c. God completes His work (3:20–21)
    4. Eternal life really is eternal life (1 John 5:13)

III. Conclusion

A. *Have You Sensed God Being at Work in Your Life?*
    1. Have you been convicted of your sins?
    2. Have you been made aware of God's love?
    3. Are you ready to come in faith to Christ?

B. *God's Good Work Can Begin in Your Life Today*

A Matter of Life or Death

Philippians 1:20–26

I. Introduction
A. *Life or Death Awaits Us Every Day*
   1. God holds our breath in His hands (Dan. 5:23)
   2. We all have an appointment with death (Heb. 9:27)
   3. The young may die; the old must die (Rom. 5:12)
B. *We Need to Be Ready to Live or Die*
C. *Paul Was Ready*

II. Body
A. *Paul's Aim, Dead or Alive (v. 20)*
   1. "Christ shall be magnified in my body"
   2. This had not always been Paul's goal
      a. Once he had taken great pride in his ancestry
      b. He had been a Pharisee . . . a religious leader
      c. Self promotion in Judaism had been his passion
      d. He had hated Christ and persecuted the church
   3. Meeting Christ on the Damascus Road changed all this (Acts 9)
   4. Now Paul endured great persecution for the cause of Christ
      a. He had been stoned, beaten, and shipwrecked
      b. He had been imprisoned; some had tried to kill him
      c. He accepted suffering to honor His Lord (2 Cor. 4:7–18)
   5. Paul counted all things but loss for Christ (Phil. 3:7–10)
   6. Magnifying Christ was the aim of Paul's life
   7. What is your aim?
B. *Paul's Assurance, Dead or Alive (vv. 21–22)*
   1. "To live is Christ, and to die is gain"
   2. Paul was convinced he couldn't lose
      a. If he lived, he would enjoy his salvation
      b. If he died, he would enjoy heaven
      c. He had two-way assurance
      d. Do you?
   3. Paul's assurance about living: Christ

       a.   Christ would be his consolation (2:1)

       b.   Christ would be his example (2:5–7)

       c.   Christ would always enable him to rejoice (3:1)

       d.   Christ would enable him to do all things (4:13)

       e.   Christ would supply all his needs (4:19)

    4.   Paul's assurance about dying: gain

    5.   Paul found it hard to choose

  C. *Paul's Anticipation, Dead or Live (vv. 23–26)*

    1.   "I am in a strait betwixt two"

    2.   Paul's first desire was to depart and be with Christ

       a.   He knew this was far better

       b.   The joys of heaven beckoned

       c.   He longed to see his Savior

    3.   Paul was also eager to keep serving Christ

       a.   "To abide in the flesh is more needful for you"

       b.   He could rejoice in the prospect of more service

       c.   He found joy in anticipating building up the church

III. Conclusion

  A. *Another Matter of Life or Death*

    1.   Are you prepared to live? to die?

    2.   No one is ready to live until ready to die

    3.   Are you ready?

  B. *You Can Have the Same Confidence About Life and Death As Paul*

The Prize

Philippians 3:13–14

I. Introduction

    A. *Most Are Interested in Prizes*
        1. Prizes represent rewards
        2. Some are earned and some are unearned
    B. *Paul Was Interested in a Prize of Great Value*
        1. A prize to be given by Jesus to the faithful
        2. A prize worth more than all earthly rewards
    C. *Paul and His Drive for the Prize*

II. Body

    A. *Paul's Past and the Prize (v. 13)*
        1. "Forgetting those things which are behind"
        2. Paul was determined not to be hindered by his past
        3. Paul regretted some things in his past
            a. His former confidence in the flesh (vv. 4–5)
            b. His hatred of Christ
            c. His persecution of the church (v. 6)
        4. Some things in his past that might have made him proud
            a. His accomplishments in the ministry
            b. The many churches he had founded
            c. His suffering as a missionary
        5. He might have felt he had done enough
        6. He determined not to look back; the prize lay ahead
    B. *Paul's Passion for the Prize (v. 13)*
        1. "Reaching forth"
        2. Paul stretching himself forward
            a. Seizing every opportunity to serve
            b. Paul felt he must give his all
            c. This was no time to become indifferent
            d. Souls were lost; there were new areas to reach
        3. Paul's passion was to accomplish God's will in his life
            a. The purpose God had for him when He saved him
            b. He kept driving himself hard to reach that goal

C. *Paul Pressing Forward toward the Mark for the Prize*
   (v. 14)
   1. "I press toward the mark"
   2. What is the mark, the goal?
      a. The example Jesus has set for us (1 Peter 2:21)
      b. Paul wanted to be like Jesus
   3. This is God's purpose in our lives
      a. Even the reason for events in our lives
         (Rom. 8:28–29)
      b. The goal of Scripture in changing our lives
   4. When will this prize be received?
      a. At the upward calling of God in Christ Jesus
      b. When Jesus returns His servants will be
         rewarded
      c. He brings the prize with Him (Rev. 22:12)

III. Conclusion

A. *How Much Thought Do You Give to Eternal Rewards?*
B. *How Focused Are You on the Prize?*
C. *What Is Hindering You in Your Quest?*
D. *Are You Looking Forward to the Upward Calling?*

Longing for Home

Philippians 3:20–21

I. **Introduction**
  A. *There's No Place Like Home*
      1. Family reunions bring us home
      2. Church homecomings bring us home
      3. The warmth and blessing of going home
  B. *This World Is Not Our Home*
      1. No wonder we sometimes long for home
      2. We're not home
  C. *Paul's Call to Look Homeward*

II. **Body**
  A. *Heaven Is Our Home (v. 20)*
      1. "Our conversation [citizenship] is in heaven"
      2. We are not citizens of earth trying to get to heaven
      3. We are citizens of heaven making our way through this earth
      4. What this meant to the Philippians
          a. Philippi was a Roman colony
          b. Roman citizenship was granted to all born there
          c. Philippians could say, "I'm a citizen of Rome"
          d. Believers there could say they were citizens of heaven
      5. We represent heaven while here on earth
          a. Let's be good ambassadors for our King (2 Cor. 5:20)
          b. Others will judge our King by how we live
      6. When born the first time we became citizens of a nation
      7. When born again we became citizens of heaven
  B. *Our King Is in Heaven (v. 20)*
      1. "From whence also we look for the Savior"
      2. The Lord Jesus Christ is our King
          a. He came down from heaven (John 3:13)
          b. He promised to prepare places in heaven (John 14:1–3)
          c. He ascended into heaven (Acts 1:9–11)

      3. We have great investments in heaven

         a. Our citizenship is there

         b. Our King is there

         c. Our inheritance is there (1 Peter 1:4)

  C. *Our King Is Coming Back to Take Us to Heaven (vv. 20–21)*

      1. We should be looking for His coming

         a. Looking for His coming purifies our lives (1 John 3:1–3)

         b. Looking for His coming adds hope to life (Titus 2:13)

      2. Christ will come and raise the Christian dead (1 Thess. 4:14)

      3. Christ will come and we will be changed (1 Cor. 15:51–52)

         a. "Who shall change our vile [lowly] body"

         b. Our bodies to be like His body (1 John 3:1)

      4. This miracle is well within the power of Christ

         a. The resurrection of His body proves His power

         b. He is in control of all things

III. Conclusion

  A. *Good Citizens of Heaven Impact Earth's Citizens for Christ*

      1. We have a world to reach (Matt. 28:18–20)

      2. We have the only message that saves (Acts 4:12)

  B. *Looking for Our Lord's Return Adds Urgency to Our Task*

How to Clean Up Our Lives

Psalms 119:9–11

I. **Introduction**
  A. *A Text with a Vital Question*
    1. How can one be clean before God?
    2. Many have asked this question
    3. What is the answer?
  B. *The Psalmist Shares His Search and Solution*

II. **Body**
  A. *The Psalmist's Desire (v. 9)*
    1. "Wherewithal shall a young man cleanse his way?"
    2. He wants to be clean
      a. He is tired of sin
      b. He is weary of broken resolutions
    3. Can you identify with this desire?
      a. Have you found yourself confessing the same sins?
      b. Do you long for daily victory?
  B. *The Scripture As a Detergent (v. 9)*
    1. "By taking heed thereto according to thy word"
    2. The blood of Christ to cleanse positionally
    3. The Bible to clean up our lives
      a. "Now ye are clean through the word" (John 15:3)
      b. "The washing of water by the word" (Eph. 5:26)
    4. The day of powerful detergents
      a. Something to clean up everything
      b. No stain too tough for modern cleansers
    5. No sin too stubborn for the Bible to eradicate
    6. Daily Bible reading is vital to daily victory over sin
  C. *The Psalmist's Decision (v. 10)*
    1. "With my whole heart have I sought thee"
    2. He hears and heeds the message for cleaning up his life
    3. He responds with his "whole heart"
      a. No hypocrisy
      b. No holding back

101

      4. God calls for surrender in the deepest part
         a. In love for God (Deut. 6:5)
         b. In faith for salvation (Rom. 10:9–13)
   D. *The Psalmist's Defense (v. 11)*
      1. "Thy word have I hid in mine heart"
      2. Spurgeon: "No cure for sin in the life is equal to the Word in the heart. There is no hiding from sin unless we hide the truth in our souls."
      3. He doesn't want to fall back into the Devil's trap
         a. He wants total victory
         b. He arms himself with the sword of the Spirit
      4. Spurgeon: "When the Word is hidden in the heart the life will be hidden from sin."

III. **Conclusion**
   A. *Do You Long to Be Clean?*
   B. *Are You Using the Divine Detergent?*
   C. *Sin Will Keep You from the Bible*
   D. *The Bible Will Keep You from Sin*

Abidlng in Christ

John 15:1–11

I. Introduction

A. *Jesus Uses Familiar Things to Explain Mysteries*
   1. Promises of mansions, the Spirit, peace
   2. The bread, the light, the door
   3. The good shepherd, the way, the truth, the life

B. *The Vine and the Branches*
   1. "Abide" used eight times in ten verses
   2. He abides in us (Rev. 3:20; Col. 1:16)
   3. We abide in Him (vv. 4–8)

C. *The Benefits of Abiding in Christ*

II. Body

A. *To Abide in Him Makes Our Prayers Effectual (v. 7)*
   1. The effectual fervent prayer of a righteous man . . . (James 5:16)
   2. Sin in the heart hinders answers to prayer (Ps. 66:18)
   3. The importance of a consistent prayer life
      a. In times of trial
      b. When a fever rages in your child
      c. When financial collapse seems imminent
      d. When health flees and strength is gone
   4. To abide in Him is always being prayed up
   5. Don't always have time to get ready for emergencies

B. *To Abide in Him Makes Our Fruit Perpetual (v. 8)*
   1. The guarantee of continual fruitfulness
      a. Further development in verses 15–17
      b. Chosen to bear fruit (v. 16)
      c. This fruit will remain (v. 16)
   2. This includes the fruit of the Spirit (Gal. 5:22–23)
   3. It also includes fruitfulness in witnessing
      a. Consistency increases the number of converts
      b. Others are observing our fruit
   4. The fruit of the Spirit in every reaction of the day
   5. We may not be aware of some fruitbearing
      a. Moses came down from Mt. Sinai with a shining face
      b. He was unaware that his face was shining

    C. *To Abide in Him Makes Our Joy Celestial (v. 11)*
- 1. Earthly obedience brings heavenly joy
- 2. "The joy that was set before Him" (Heb. 12:2)
- 3. Paul and Silas were even joyful in prison (Acts 16:25–32)
  - a. Heavenly joy in a dungeon
  - b. Heavenly joy with their backs bruised and bleeding
  - c. Heavenly joy at midnight
  - d. Heavenly joy that caused an earthquake
- 4. Believers are earth's examples of heaven's joy
- 5. This joy remains in us
- 6. This is fullness of joy

III. Conclusion
    A. *A Call to the Abiding Life*
- 1. Confession of all sin
- 2. Constant communion with Christ

    B. *All These Blessings Are the One Who Calls Us Friends (v. 15)*

    C. *Abiding in Jesus We Are Closer Than Earthly Friends Can Ever Be*

The Lord's Prayer

Matthew 6:9–15

I. **Introduction**
   A. *Sixty-Six Familiar Words*
      1. Quoted by millions
      2. Sometimes in a great blending of voices
      3. Sometimes alone in a closet
   B. *Why We Have the Lord's Prayer*
      1. In answer to the disciples' plea: "Teach us to pray"
      2. Perhaps should be called "The disciples' prayer"
   C. *What Is This Pattern Prayer All About?*

II. **Body**
   A. *A Prayer That Calls for a Relationship with the Father*
      1. "Our Father"
      2. What a tender word!
         a. The many memories of fathers
         b. "A father of the fatherless" (Ps. 68:5)
         c. "As a father pitieth his children" (Ps. 103:13)
         d. "The everlasting Father" (Isa. 9:6)
      3. Only a believer can call God "Father"
      4. Jesus came to bring people into the family of God
      5. John R. Rice: "Our position as born–again sons with a loving Father should make us confident and bold in our praying."
   B. *A Prayer That Calls for Reverence Toward God*
      1. "Hallowed be thy name"
      2. We should approach God with worship and adoration
      3. Reverence is more than being quiet in church
      4. Reverence is more than being solemn during the Prelude
      5. Reverence is recognizing the holiness of God (Isa. 6:1–6)
      6. Reverence is an acknowledgement of personal sin
      7. Reverence is faith in our holy and loving God
      8. Reverence is living carefully because God is holy
   C. *A Prayer That Calls for the Return of the Lord*
      1. "Thy kingdom come"

105

2. Praying this prayer is praying for Christ's return
   a. The disciples expected the kingdom then
   b. They thought the world was ready
   c. The world is more ready now than then
3. Christ will come and set up His kingdom
   a. There will be peace over all the earth
   b. The earth will be filled with the knowledge of the Lord
   c. The enmity between people and animals will end
   d. The desert will blossom as a rose
   e. The earth will produce abundant crops
4. Each Communion service we look forward to the kingdom

III. Conclusion
A. *What a Wonderful Pattern Prayer!*
   1. Can you pray the Lord's prayer?
   2. Are you one of His children? (John 1:12)
B. *Are You Ready for the Return of Our Lord?*

The Last Prayer in the Bible

Revelation 22:20

I. **Introduction**
   A. *The Last Invitation in the Bible (22:17)*
      1. An invitation for all to come to Christ
      2. A call for all to call "Come!"
   B. *The Last Prayer in the Bible Is Also an Invitation to Come*
      1. Not an invitation to people but to Christ
      2. Should be always on the lips of every Christian
   C. *What Is the Last Prayer in the Bible?*

II. **Body**
   A. *A Prayer for the Immediate Return of Christ*
      1. "Even so"
      2. A response to "Surely I come quickly"
      3. This prayer starts with "Amen"
      4. A prayer that accepts Christ's return by faith
      5. All things about Christ must be taken by faith
         a. Old Testament prophets looked forward in faith
         b. His birth, death, and resurrection fulfilled
      6. The Lord's return promised to be sudden (Matt. 24:37–44)
         a. "Watch therefore" (Matt. 25:13)
         b. "In a moment" (1 Cor. 15:51–52)
   B. *A Prayer for the Interruption of Our Present Plans*
      1. "Come"
      2. We all make plans for the future
         a. Places we plan to go
         b. Things we plan to accomplish
         c. How to temper our plans (the Lord's will) (James 4:13–15)
      3. Other interruptions to our plans
         a. Death
         b. Disaster
         c. Illness
      4. This prayer asks for a better interruption
      5. This prayer gives Christ's return priority

          a.   More important than all our plans
          b.   More important than all our goals
      6.   How important is the return of Christ to you?
      7.   Do you want Him to return quickly?
  C. *A Prayer for a Personal Meeting with Christ*
      1.   "Lord Jesus"
      2.   Face-to-face with Christ our Savior
      3.   John's conclusion after viewing the future
          a.   "Even so, come Lord Jesus"
          b.   John was eager for Christ to come
          c.   Are you eager for Christ to come?
      4.   This is the "blessed hope"
      5.   Is Christ's coming your hope?

III. Conclusion
  A. *What the Return of Christ Will Mean*
      1.   The resurrection of the dead in Christ
      2.   The rapture of living believers
      3.   The receiving of rewards
      4.   Time with Jesus in heaven
  B. *Is the Last Prayer in the Bible Your Prayer?*
  C. *If So, It Will Purify Your Life (1 John 2:1–3)*

A Nation in Need

Exodus 32:1–8

I. Introduction

A. *God and the History of Nations*
1. God is at work in all nations
2. God and our independence
   a. His faithfulness in the early years
   b. His guidance for the struggling founders
   c. His leading in forming a land of religious liberty
3. God and His work in Israel
   a. Their deliverance from Egypt
   b. A nation to give His Word to the world

B. *The Tragic Scene*
1. Moses on Mt. Sinai receiving the law
2. The impatience, the complaining, the golden calf

C. *Parallels of Israel's Needs and Ours*

II. Body

A. *Their Need to Remember Their Past (v. 1)*
1. The difficult days in Egypt (3:7–8)
   a. They had been slaves of cruel taskmasters
   b. Their sons were drowned at birth
   c. They had cried out to God for deliverance
2. America's humble beginnings
   a. The courage needed to declare independence
   b. The military odds against gaining independence
   c. Freedom seemed an impossible dream to some
3. Washington praying at Valley Forge
4. An independent and free nation is born

B. *Their Need to Remember God's Provision (v. 4)*
1. God provided a deliverer
   a. Moses and the burning bush (Exod. 3:2–4)
   b. "I am come down to deliver them" (3:8)
2. The plagues brought on Egypt to free them
3. The passover; the opening of the Red Sea; the cloud and fire
4. Angel's food (manna) and water from a rock

      5. God's great provisions for us
        a. Victory in the Revolutionary War
        b. Preserving the union during the Civil War
        c. Bountiful harvests, prosperity, abundant blessings

  C. *Their Need to Remember God's Purpose (vv. 7–8)*
      1. To be God's people (Exod. 6:7)
        a. To be a witness to other nations
        b. To give His Word to the world
        c. To receive the land promised them (6:8)
      3. God has had a purpose for America
        a. A place where people could worship Him freely
        b. A nation to send missionaries around the world
        c. A nation that would befriend His people, Israel

III. Conclusion
  A. *Remembering Brings Us Back to Basics*
      1. We recall God at work in our lives
      2. We recall commitments we made to Him
  B. *The Basics of Freedom*
      1. Freedom flows from the Bible (John 8:32)
      2. Freedom comes from the Savior (John 8:36)
  C. *America Needs to Get Back to Basics*

Let Us Return to the Lord

Hosea 6:1

I. **Introduction**
   A. *Hosea's Call to Repentance*
      1. "Come, and let us return unto the LORD"
      2. He hath torn, and he will heal us
      3. He hath smitten, and he will bind us up
   B. *A Call of Hope to a Troubled Nation*
      1. The nation was in moral and religious decay
      2. Hosea offers healing and help to troubled people
   C. *Why These People Needed to Return to the Lord*

II. **Body**
   A. *They Had Departed from the Lord in Their Worship (4:1)*
      1. Hosea minces no words: speaks bluntly
      2. The Lord's controversy with the people
         a. No truth in the land
         b. No mercy in the land
         c. No knowledge of God in the land
      3. Truth grows out of being right with God (John 8:32)
      4. Mercy flows from knowing our merciful God (Ps. 103:17)
      5. God's people had forsaken Him
         a. They had no time for Him
         b. Lesser things had all their adoration
      6. The nation was in need of a great revival
         a. Worship had become formalistic
         b. Worship was not a life-changing experience
         c. Their worship lacked faith
      7. Could this be a commentary on our country today?
   B. *They Had Departed from the Lord in Their Words (4:2)*
      1. "By swearing and lying"
      2. Words measure our spiritual condition
         a. They reveal what occupies the mind
         b. They reveal the state of the heart (Matt. 12:33–37)
      3. The people had made profanity their practice

a. Profanity is one of the marks of decadence
b. "Put . . . filthy communication out of your mouth" (Col. 3:8)
4. Lying is not to be taken lightly
a. Satan is a liar (John 8:44)
b. Believers are to put away lying (Eph. 4:25)
5. A good verse to eliminate swearing and lying (Ps. 19:14)

C. *They Had Departed from the Lord in Their Works (4:2)*
1. Three marks of decay in Israel at that time
a. Killing (Exod. 20:13)
b. Stealing (Exod. 20:15)
c. Committing adultery (Exod. 20:14)
2. All of these forbidden by the Scriptures
3. These sins are prevalent in America today
a. Killing brings danger to our streets and homes
b. Stealing costs us all
c. Committing adultery increases disease and ruins marriages

III. Conclusion
A. *The People Invited to Return to the Lord*
1. Return in spite of their sins
2. Return and be forgiven
B. *God Still Calls the Wayward to Return*
C. *He Will Pardon, Cleanse, and Revive (6:2)*

How God Speaks

Hebrews 1:1–3

I. **Introduction**
   A. *An Old Puritan Preacher's Two Questions*
      1. Does God speak?
      2. What does He say?
   B. *Man Certainly Speaks*
      1. Much of what he says is not worth saying
      2. How strange our endless chatter must sound to the angels
   C. *God Has Spoken and Is Still Speaking*

II. **Body**
   A. *God Spoke in the Past by the Prophets (v. 1)*
      1. God has not been silent
         a. He has spoken by the prophets
         b. The Old Testament authenticated
      2. How God spoke to the prophets
         a. Sometimes through angels, as to Abraham (Gen. 18)
         b. Sometimes directly, as to Moses (Exod. 3)
         c. Sometimes through creation, as to David (Ps. 8)
         d. Sometimes through visions, as to Daniel (Dan. 7)
         e. Always by the Holy Spirit (2 Peter 1:21)
      3. The many prophecies fulfilled and being fulfilled
         a. Prophecies about the birth of Christ
         b. Prophecies about the death and resurrection of Christ
         c. Prophecies about the return of Christ
         d. Prophecies about the kingdom of Christ
         e. Prophecies about the movements of nations
         f. Prophecies about the future of Israel
   B. *God Has Spoken in These Last Days (v. 2)*
      1. "In these last days"
         a. From Pentecost to the Kingdom (Acts 2:17)
         b. He is speaking to us now
      2. God is not silent in any age

3. Prophetic developments through which He is speaking
   a. The knowledge explosion (Dan. 12:4)
   b. New diseases (Matt. 24:7)
   c. Signs in nature: earthquakes, etc. (Matt. 24:7)
   d. Moral decline (Matt. 24:12)
   e. Technology preparing for the Antichrist (Rev. 13)
   f. The return of the Jews to their homeland (Ezek. 37)
4. God's prophetic plan is being fulfilled
5. What a great time to be alive!

C. *God Has Spoken to Us Through His Son (vv. 2–3)*
1. Everything we need to know is in Jesus
2. Do you want to know about God's grace? Study Jesus!
3. Do you want to know about God's love? Study Jesus!
4. Do you want to know about God's power? Study Jesus!
5. Do you want to know about God's wisdom? Study Jesus!
6. Do you want to know about the future? Study Jesus!

III. **Conclusion**
A. *William R. Newell on This Text*
1. "Christ Himself, the Son of God, is God's message"
2. "Christ is . . . the personal Voice and eternal gift of God"

B. *God Is Speaking to You about Jesus Putting Away Your Sins (v. 3)*
C. *What Is Your Answer to Him?*

Winning over Temptation

1 Corinthians 10:13

I. Introduction
  A. *Why Temptation Troubles Us All*
  1. All are targets of the tempter
  2. All feel the lure of the world
  3. All experience the appetites of the flesh
  B. *A Text to Bring Victory to the Tempted*

II. Body
  A. *The Tempter We Face*
  1. We have an adversary (1 Peter 5:8)
     a. Satan is compared to a roaring lion
     b. He continually seeks victims
  2. Satan is the source of temptation
     a. Temptation in the Garden of Eden (Gen. 3)
     b. The temptation of Jesus (Matt. 4)
  3. The Tempter is a deceiver (2 Cor. 11:3)
  4. The Tempter is a liar (John 8:44)
  5. The Tempter is a thief (John 10:10)
  6. We are equipped to win over this powerful enemy (1 John 4:4)
     a. The Holy Spirit is within every believer
     b. The Holy Spirit is greater in power than our foe
  B. *The Lord Who Is Faithful*
  1. "God is faithful"
  2. God limits temptation to such as is common to man
     a. Satan is allowed no untried enticements
     b. The world is allowed no unknown allurements
     c. The flesh is allowed no unexperienced cravings
  3. Others have been tempted as you are today
     a. Some have lost the battle
     b. Others have won
     c. You can win
  4. God limits temptation to what we can resist
     a. Temptation cannot be "above what you are able"

         b.   Don't say resisting is impossible for you

         c.   God guarantees you are up to the occasion

         d.   His grace is sufficient for today's test

    C.   *The Way of Escape We Must Find*

       1.   Every temptation is required to have a way of escape

       2.   This is a Divinely prepared escape route

         a.   God will always "make a way of escape"

         b.   This is His way of showing His love

       3.   Escape routes God has furnished for others who were tempted

         a.   A timely phone call

         b.   A Scripture verse brought to mind

         c.   The appearance of a helpful person

       4.   On the darkest day, God makes a way

III.   Conclusion

    A.   *Are You Enduring Temptation Today?*

       1.   Are you near defeat?

       2.   Are you about to yield to the tempter?

    B.   *You Can Triumph over This Temptation*

       1.   Our Lord has faced the tempter and defeated him

       2.   He will give strength and grace for you to triumph too

The Hot Rod Who Was Used of God

I. **Introduction**
   A. *What We Know About Jehu*
      1. First mentioned in connection with Elijah
         (1 Kings 19:16)
      2. The discouraged prophet was to make three
         appointments
         a. Hazael was to be anointed king over Syria
         b. Jehu was to be anointed king over Israel
         c. Elisha was to be anointed prophet in Elijah's
            place
      3. We also know that Jehu was a fast driver
         (2 Kings 9:20)
   B. *The Work God Gave Jehu to Do*
      1. He was to destroy the house of Ahab
      2. He was to root out evil in the land
   C. *Jehu Invites Jehonadab to Join Him in Completing His
      Work*
      1. Jehu's moving words to Jehonadab
      2. Good words for any to seek to serve the Lord

II. **Body**
   A. *Hearts Right (v. 15)*
      1. "Is thine heart right, as my heart is with thy heart?"
      2. The first requirement for doing the work of God
      3. Our hearts are not naturally right
         a. "Deceitful and desperately wicked" (Jer. 17:9)
         b. Evil proceeds out of the heart (Matt. 15:19)
         c. Christ changes us (2 Cor 5:17)
      4. Great heart possibilities
         a. God can search the heart (Jer. 17:10)
         b. God's Word discerns the heart (Heb. 4:12)
         c. Christ can knock on the heart's door
            (Rev. 3:20)
         d. We can believe with the heart (Rom. 10:10)
         e. God's love can be shed abroad in the heart
            (Rom. 5:5)
         f. God's Word can be hidden in the heart
            (Ps. 119:11)

117

        g. God's gladness can be in the heart (Ps. 4:7)

    5. Hindrances to having our hearts right

        a. Sin (Ps. 66:18)

        b. Hardening (Rom. 2:5)

        c. Slow to believe (Luke 24:25)

    6. When the heart is right we are ready to serve God

B. *Hands Together (v. 15)*

    1. "Give me thine hand"

    2. A sincere invitation for working together

    3. Bible examples and exhortations for working together

        a. How good and pleasant (Ps. 133)

        b. All of one accord (Acts 1:14; 2:1)

        c. Be of one mind (Phil. 2:2)

    4. The power of a united church

C. *Holy Zeal (v. 16)*

    1. "See my zeal for the LORD"

    2. We could use some holy zeal in the churches today

    3. The church at Laodicea was lukewarm, a disappointment

    4. We need churches that are zealous for Christ, on fire

III. Conclusion

A. *Let Us Get Our Hearts Right and Our Hands Together*

B. *Let the Community See Our Zeal for the Lord*

C. *We Have Work to Do for Our King*

"It is far better to have zeal without knowledge than to have knowledge without zeal."   —D. L. Moody

Preparing for Trouble

John 16:33

I. Introduction

A. *Dark Days Were Ahead for the Disciples*
1. The betrayal of Christ by Judas
2. The trial when they would forsake Him and flee
3. Peter's denials of Christ
4. The crucifixion and death of Christ

B. *Jesus Prepared the Disciples for These Coming Dark Days*
1. He told them about heaven (John 14:1–3)
2. He told them about the Holy Spirit (John 14:16–27)
3. He called them His friends (John 15:13–15)

C. *Why Do These Teachings Bring Peace in Troubled Times?*

II. Body

A. *How Does the Hope of Heaven Bring Us Peace (John 14:1–3)?*
1. We all have trouble here
   a. "In the world ye shall have tribulation"
   b. We share in the troubles of this world
2. Believers find peace by taking the long look
   a. All trials are temporary
   b. We must look beyond them
   c. The best is yet to come
3. "Let not your heart be troubled"
   a. Misery here but mansions ahead
   b. Pain here but prepared places ahead
4. We put up with contrary people here
5. We'll spend eternity with Christ later
6. Others may desert us but Christ is coming for us

B. *How Can the Holy Spirit Bring Us Peace (14:16–27)?*
1. Jesus called the Holy Spirit the Comforter
   a. He comforts us when we are distressed
   b. He comforts us when we feel like caving in
2. The Holy Spirit dwells within every Christian
   a. Comfort is available from Him all the time
   b. He teaches us faith building truth
   c. As faith increases fear decreases

    3.   The Holy Spirit reminds us of God's faithfulness

C. *How Does Being a Friend of Jesus Provide Peace (John 15:13–15)?*
    1.   Friends are close in times of need
        a.   Jesus is as close as a vine to its branches
        b.   Jesus is so close that we abide in Him
        c.   Jesus is closer than a brother or sister
    2.   This Friend loves us (15:13)
        a.   He has died for us
        b.   He calls us His friends
    3.   This friend will never forsake us (Heb. 13:5)
        a.   The disciples abandoned Him and fled
        b.   He remained faithful to them
        c.   He will remain faithful to us

III.   Conclusion
    A. *In This World We Will Have Trouble*
    B. *In Christ We Can Have Peace*
    C. *Christ Has Overcome the World*
    D. *Trusting Him We Are Also Overcomers*

Losing and Finding

Matthew 16:25–26

I. Introduction
    A. *Jesus Took His Disciples on a Retreat*
        1. Caesarea-Philippi, north of the Jordan valley
        2. A beautiful place to come apart
        3. If we don't come apart, we'll come apart
    B. *Revelations on This Retreat*
        1. The revelation of the church
        2. The revelation of the cross
        3. The revelation of losing and finding
           a. What this meant to the disciples
           b. What this means to you and me

II. Body
    A. *Saving Is Losing (v. 25)*
        1. "Whosoever will save his life"
        2. In giving all to Christ we gain
           a. This is hard for human nature to grasp
           b. The rich young ruler didn't understand it
           c. King Agrippa almost understood it
               (Acts 26:28)
        3. In holding back from full surrender we lose
           a. This principle is true even in salvation
           b. Salvation cannot be part works and part grace
           c. Christ must be all or nothing at all
    B. *Losing Is Finding (v. 25)*
        1. "Whosoever will lose his life . . ."
        2. Seeing through the deceitfulness of sin
        3. Coming to a life changing decision
        4. Consider Moses choosing to identify with God's people
           a. He lost his position in Egypt (Heb. 11:24–25)
           b. He gained a place in God's plan (Heb. 11:26)
        5. Here is Nicodemas coming to Jesus by night
        6. Here are the disciples leaving all to follow Christ
        7. Here is Saul becoming Paul the missionary
        8. What have you lost for Jesus?
        9. Losing temporal things for Him brings great eternal gain

    C. *Profit Is Loss (v. 26)*
        1. "What is a man profited . . . ?"
        2. This may be the most difficult lesson to learn
           a. The world is so alluring
           b. We see the world but cannot see the soul
           c. Most people are trying to gain the world
        3. Is some earthly goal keeping you from Christ?
        4. Jesus placed infinite value on the human soul
        5. How valuable is your soul to you?
        6. Consider the cross to see the value of a soul to Jesus
           a. The nails, the thorns, the pain, all for souls
           b. The shedding of His blood on the cross for souls

III. Conclusion
    A. *This Is a Sermon About Unconditional Surrender*
        1. Are you willing to count all but loss for Christ?
        2. Are you keeping back some area of your life from Him?
    B. *Remember Losing Is Finding*
    C. *Surrender All to Him Today*

Accepting a New Challenge in Life

Joshua 1:1–6

I. Introduction
A. *A Chapter Closes at the Opening of This Book*
1. Moses is dead
   a. Moses, who had led his people out of slavery
   b. Moses, who had received the law from God
2. This symbolized the end of the dispensation of law
   a. "The law was given by Moses" (John 1:17)
   b. Joshua a type of Christ . . . followed Moses
   c. "Grace and truth came by Jesus Christ" (John 1:17)
3. A new chapter opens in Joshua's life

II. Body
A. *The Commission (vv. 2–4)*
1. "Go over this Jordan"
   a. Joshua to lead his people
   b. Moses had said this day would come (Deut. 31:1–8)
2. How big are your feet, Joshua? (vv. 3–4)
   a. Every place Joshua walked was to be given to him
   b. Joshua had walked here before as a spy (Num. 13:8)
   c. He had seen the bounty of this good land (Num. 13:21–25)
3. The good report of Joshua and Caleb then (Num. 14:6–9)
4. But the doubters had won the day
5. Now Joshua will lead the conquest of Canaan
B. *The Conflict (v. 4)*
1. Canaan was occupied
   a. The inhabitants were very strong
   b. A major problem: the walled city of Jericho
2. The conflicts of the Christian life
   a. Conflict with the world (1 John 2:15–17)
   b. Conflict with the flesh (Gal. 5:19–21)
   c. Conflict with the Devil (Eph. 6:10–18)

123

3. Has the conflict been difficult for you today?
4. Redpath: "Are you in the wilderness of defeat, or in the land of victory? Is your life a constant struggle against the powers of darkness, with constant defeat, or is it a victorious war waged in the power of a Risen Lord?"

C. *The Call for Courage (v. 6)*
   1. "Be strong and of a good courage"
   2. Reasons Joshua might have been afraid
      a. He was beginning a new vocation
      b. He had been given a staggering responsibility
      c. His hero had died
      d. He was not young
   3. Reasons for courage
      a. The power of God
      b. The presence of God
      c. The promises of God
   4. Joshua was equipped to win the conflict and so are we

III. Conclusion

A. *Our Lord Has Good Things Ahead for His People*
   1. Salvation is only the beginning
   2. Great victories are ours for the taking
B. *Let's March Forward in Faith*
C. *No Enemy Can Stand Against Us*
D. *Our Victorious Savior Will Lead Us All the Way*

The Fruit of the Spirit Is Love

Series on the Fruit of the Spirit Begins   *Galatians 5:22*

I. Introduction
   A. *Paul's Advice to a Troubled Church*
      1. A church that had become legalistic
      2. Paul called them back to grace
   B. *Paul Reminds Them of the Holy Spirit and the Christian Life*
      1. The work of the Spirit in conversion (3:3)
      2. The fruit of the Spirit should follow (5:22–23)
   C. *The Series on the Fruit of the Spirit*
   D. *The Fruit of the Spirit Is Love*

II. Body
   A. *Love for God*
      1. How natural this should be
      2. The great commandment (Matt. 22:37)
      3. Evidences that people do not love God
         a. Use of His name in vain
         b. Lack of appreciation for His blessings
         c. Lives given to the works of the flesh
      4. The change when conversion takes place
         a. A new awareness of God's love
         b. "We love him because he first loved us" (1 John 4:19)
      5. A believer's love for God may cool (Rev. 2:1–5)
      6. What is the temperature of your love?
   B. *Love for the Family of God*
      1. We are born into God's family by faith in Christ
         a. A whole company of brothers and sisters
         b. A unique new relationship
      2. Proofs of new life
         a. "Love one to another" (John 13:34–35)
         b. "We love the brethren" (1 John 3:14)
      3. The lack of love shown in many churches
      4. The Galatians had once loved one another
         a. When legalism came, love left
         b. Now they were destroying one another (5:15)
      5. Paul longed to see love flowing through them again

C. *Love for the Lost*
1. The Holy Spirit causes us to be like Jesus
2. The Lord and His love for sinners
    a. He came to seek and save the lost (Luke 19:10)
    b. He was criticized for loving sinners (Luke 15:2)
    c. His death for sinners proved His love (Rom. 5:8)
3. Spirit filled people love sinners and minister to them

III. Conclusion
A. *Summarizing Evidences of the Spirit Filled Life*
1. Love for God
2. Love for the family of God
3. Love for the lost
B. *How Shall We Recognize This Love?*
1. It is more than sentimental feelings
2. It is described in 1 Cor. 13
C. *Yield Completely to the Holy Spirit*
D. *His Love Will Flow Through You Every Day*

The Fruit of the Spirit Is Joy

I. **Introduction**
   A. *The War Within Us (vv. 16–17)*
      1. The war between the flesh and the Spirit
      2. A war that begins when one is born again
      3. Paul writes from experience (Rom. 7)
      4. He found victory in yielding to the Holy Spirit (Rom. 8)
   B. *Looking at the Fruit of the Spirit*
      1. The fruit of the Spirit is love: last sermon
      2. The fruit of the Spirit is joy

II. **Body**
   A. *The Joy of Salvation (Ps. 51:12)*
      1. David wrote with a burdened heart
         a. He had lost the joy of salvation
         b. He longed to have it again
      2. The joy of knowing sins are forgiven (1 John 1:7)
      3. The joy of being a child of God (John 1:12)
      4. The joy of knowing heaven is ahead (Phil. 1:21–23)
      5. The joy of being at peace with God (Rom. 5:1)
   B. *The Joy of a Fruitful Life (John 15:11)*
      1. We need to evaluate our spiritual condition often
      2. Is the joy of the Lord our daily experience?
         a. If not, why not?
         b. What needs to be corrected?
      3. Are we abiding in Christ?
         a. Fully surrendered to Him
         b. Keeping a strong devotional life
         c. Feeding on God's Word daily
         d. Confessing all known sin
      4. The moving account of the vine and the branches
         a. Are we drawing daily life from Jesus?
         b. Are we bearing fruit for Him?
   C. *The Joy of Answered Prayer (John 16:24)*
      1. The Holy Spirit and our prayer life
         a. He leads us to pray (Rom. 8:14)
         b. He directs us when we pray (Rom. 8:15)

        c.   He bears witness when we pray (Rom. 8:16)

        d.   He intercedes when we don't know how to pray (Rom. 8:26)

    2.   Joy increases when we pray in the name of Jesus

    3.   Joy accompanies answers to prayer

D. *The Joy of Leading Others to Christ (1 Thess. 2:19)*

    1.   This is one of the reasons for Heaven's joy

    2.   This brings joy to the angels (Luke 15:7, 10)

    3.   This made the cross bearable for Jesus (Heb. 12:2)

    4.   The blessed cycle of joy

        a.   The joyful Spirit-filled life produces converts

        b.   Seeing fruit from witnessing increases joy

III. Conclusion

A. *Spirit-Produced Joy Cannot Be Worked Up*

    1.   The fruit of the Spirit comes from within

    2.   The Holy Spirit is within every child of God

B. *Stop Grieving the Holy Spirit (Eph. 4:30)*

C. *Stop Quenching the Holy Spirit (1 Thess. 5:19)*

D. *Experience the Joy of the Lord*

The Fruit of the Spirit Is Peace

Series on the Fruit of the Spirit   *Galatians 5:22*

I. Introduction

    A. *What Good Fruit the Holy Spirit Produces*
        1. Love, joy, peace, all enrich our lives
        2. God wants to do good things in us

    B. *Fruit and Works Contrasted*
        1. Works come from fleshly effort
        2. Fruit grows from life within

    C. *The Holy Spirit Wants to Bring Peace to Your Life*

II. Body

    A. *Peace with God (Rom. 5:1)*
        1. We are not naturally at peace with God
            a. Sin broke the peaceful relationship of Eden
            b. This is why the world is in trouble
        2. The search for peace
            a. Trying to find peace in pleasure
            b. Trying to find peace in entertainment
            c. Trying to find peace in substances (alcohol, drugs)
            d. Trying to find peace in financial security
        3. There is no peace apart from God (Isa. 57:19–21)
        4. Christ came to bring us peace
            a. He died for sinners (Rom. 5:6–9)
            b. He is the source of peace (Eph. 2:13–17)
        5. One step further
            a. Some have peace with God but do not feel peaceful
            b. Peace with God should not be limited to position
            c. Peace with God should be our daily experience

    B. *The Peace of God (Phil. 4:6–7)*
        1. This is peace in all circumstances
            a. When things aren't going well
            b. When anxiety would otherwise replace peace
        2. Peace when funds are low and debts are high
        3. Peace when health is uncertain
        4. Peace when storms are raging

      5. God's formula for this kind of peace
         a. Prayer: the Holy Spirit prompts prayer
         b. Thanksgiving: the Holy Spirit produces thanksgiving
         c. Faith: the Holy Spirit gives faith

  C. *Peace with Others (Eph. 4:1–3)*
      1. The Holy Spirit breaks down barriers between believers
      2. "The unity of the Spirit in the bond of peace"
         a. This is always characteristic of revival
         b. Consider the early church (Acts 1:14; 2:1)
      3. Things that grieve the Holy Spirit (Eph. 4:30)
         a. Bitterness
         b. Anger
         c. Evil speaking
      4. The Holy Spirit can mend your relationships

III. Conclusion

  A. *Quench Not the Spirit*
      1. Stop resisting the Holy Spirit
      2. Be sensitive to His voice
  B. *Allow the Holy Spirit's Peace to Rule in Your Heart*

The Fruit of the Spirit Is Longsuffering (Patience)

Series on the Fruit of the Spirit   *Galatians 5:22*

I. Introduction
    A. *One of the Most Needed Fruits to Bear*
        1. Patience doesn't come easy for most people
        2. Calls for giving the Holy Spirit complete control
    B. *Review of the Series*
        1. The fruit of the Spirit is love
        2. The fruit of the Spirit is joy
        3. The fruit of the Spirit is peace
    C. *Patience and the Christian Life*

II. Body
    A. *Exhortations to Patience*
        1. God often calls on us to wait
            a. "Wait on the Lord" (Ps. 27:14)
            b. "Wait patiently for him" (Ps. 37:7)
            c. "Wait only upon God" (Ps. 62:5)
            d. "They that wait upon the Lord" (Isa. 40:31)
            e. "The Lord is good to them that wait for him" (Lam. 3:25)
        3. The disciples to wait for the Holy Spirit (Acts 1:4)
        4. We are to "wait for his Son from heaven" (1 Thess. 1:10)
        5. Christians to run the race "with patience" (Heb. 12:1)
    B. *Examples of Patience*
        1. Job is the most common example
            a. Patient when his family and fortune were taken
            b. Patient when his wife urged him to curse God and die
        2. The patience of Shadrach, Meshach, and Abednego (Dan. 3)
        3. The patience of Daniel in the lion's den (Dan. 6)
        4. The patience of Paul and Silas in prison (Acts 16:25–32)
        5. Jesus was the greatest example of patience
            a. His patience before Pilate

      b. His patience on the cross
      c. His patience in returning (2 Peter 3:9)
  C. *Excellent Opportunities to Witness Through Patience*
    1. Patient husbands may win their wives
    2. Patient wives may win their husbands
    3. Patient employers may win their employees
    4. Patient drivers impress other drivers
    5. Patient people stand out in a crowd
    6. Observers of patient people wonder how they can do it
      a. They believe their witness is real
      b. Opportunities like these worth waiting for
    7. Others see the Holy Spirit at work through patient people

III. Conclusion

  A. *You Can Be Patient*
    1. The Holy Spirit will calm you down
    2. Your patience depends on your degree of surrender
  B. *See How the Fruit of the Spirit Progresses*
    1. Love, joy, peace, patience
    2. Each is strengthened by the others
    3. All flow from love

The Fruit of the Spirit Is Gentleness (Kindness)

Series on the Fruit of the Spirit   *Galatians 5:22*

I. **Introduction**
   A. *Important Facts about the Holy Spirit*
      1. The Holy Spirit is God
      2. The Holy Spirit brings us to Christ
      3. The Holy Spirit lives within each Christian
   B. *How to Be Filled with the Holy Spirit*
      1. Stop grieving the Spirit (Eph. 4:30)
      2. Stop quenching the Spirit (1 Thess. 5:19)
      3. Start walking in the Spirit (Gal. 5:16)
   C. *The Fruit of the Spirit Should Be Evident in Us*
   D. *The Fruit of the Spirit Is Kindness*

II. **Body**
   A. *Kindness in the Scriptures*
      1. God's kindness to us
         a. "A God of great kindness" (Neh. 9:17)
         b. "His marvelous kindness" (Ps. 31:21)
         c. "His merciful kindness" (Ps. 117:2)
         d. "His lovingkindness (Ps. 103:4)
         e. "Everlasting kindness" (Isa. 54:8)
      2. Our kindness to others
         a. As a demonstration of love (1 Cor. 13:4)
         b. As a result of not grieving the Spirit
            (Eph. 4:32)
         c. Advice to the Romans (Rom. 12:10)
         d. As an evidence of Christian growth
            (2 Peter 1:7)
   B. *Kindness in Our Speech*
      1. A very important place for kindness
      2. Speech as a test of genuine Christianity
         (James 3:2)
      3. The contradiction of kind and cutting words
         (James 3:9)
         a. "Therewith bless we God"
         b. "Therewith curse we men"
      4. Harshness of speech so harmful to the cause of
         Christ

133

        a. Harsh words that cannot be recalled
        b. Harsh words that wound those we love
        c. Harsh words that divide churches
    5. Kind words come from the Holy Spirit
        a. Words of comfort
        b. Words of encouragement
        c. Words that build faith

  C. *Kindness with Our Substance*
    1. The example of the early church (Acts 2:44–45)
    2. Paul's collections for the saints (1 Cor. 16:1)
    3. Kindness in giving called for in the Bible
        a. "Give to him that asketh" (Matt. 5:25)
        b. "A cup of cold water" (Mark 9:41)
        c. "Give to him that needeth" (Eph. 4:28)
    4. Kindness is another dimension of love

III. Conclusion
  A. *Kindness Reveals Our Degree of Surrender to the Lord*
  B. *Selfishness Reveals Our Degree of Carnality*
  C. *Do Others See the Kindness of Christ in Us?*
  D. *Love, Joy, Peace, Patience, Kindness*
    1. Goals of the Holy Spirit for you and me
    2. Developing the character of Christ in us all

The Fruit of the Spirit Is Goodness

Series on the Fruit of the Spirit   *Galatians 5:22*

I. Introduction

   A. *The Fruit of the Spirit and Human Failure*
      1. Love, joy, peace, patience, kindness, goodness
      2. Higher standards than we can achieve
      3. The Holy Spirit produces them in us
   B. *Not the Works of the Spirit But the Fruit of the Spirit*
      1. Salvation is not reformation but regeneration
      2. Changes in us are not due to imitation but indwelling power
      3. The Holy Spirit is doing good things in us
   C. *Recognizing Goodness*

II. Body

   A. *A Good Disposition*
      1. This is different than a good mood
         a. Moods come and go
         b. Moods are changeable, like the weather
      2. A good disposition is a part of personality
         a. But this is more than an inherited trait
         b. This is living consistent with God's love
         c. It is loving others as God loves us
      3. A good disposition makes us easy to live with
      4. A good disposition makes us approachable every day
      5. A good disposition shows love, joy, peace, patience, kindness
   B. *A Good Attitude*
      1. This is amiability *(Pulpit Commentary)*
      2. A Spirit filled person is friendly
      3. Are you friendly?
      4. Jesus was quick to befriend the needy
         a. He was a friend of sinners
         b. Always reaching out to hurting ones
      5. Looking for the best in people
         a. Not focusing on faults
         b. Not complaining, not slandering
      6. Do you need a better attitude at home, at church, at work?

   C. *A Desire to Do Good to Others*
      1. Good works do not earn salvation (Eph. 2:8–9)
         a. We are saved by grace through faith
         b. We cannot earn heaven through good works
      2. Good works are to be the evidence of new life
         a. "Created unto good works" (Eph. 2:10)
         b. "Faith without works is dead" (James 2:26)
      3. Seizing opportunities to do good to others
         a. Visiting the sick
         b. Caring for widows
         c. Giving to the poor
         d. Comforting those who are grieving
         e. Bearing one another's burdens

III. Conclusion
   A. *Time for a Checkup*
      1. Checking your disposition
      2. Checking your attitude
      3. Checking your service for others
   B. *What Changes Need to Be Made?*
   C. *Let the Holy Spirit Make Them*

The Fruit of the Spirit Is Faith

Series on the Fruit of the Spirit   *Galatians 5:22*

I. **Introduction**
   A. *The Work of the Holy Spirit*
      1. You are here because of His work
      2. If a lost person, His work is to bring you to Christ
      3. If a believer, His work brought about your new birth
      4. If a backslider, His work is to restore
   B. *The Believer's Body Is the Temple of the Holy Spirit*
      1. His presence within revealed by the fruit He produces
      2. The fruit of the Spirit is faith

II. **Body**
   A. *Faith That Is Childlike (Matt. 18:1–4)*
      1. Some try to make faith complicated
      2. Jesus illustrated faith with a little child
         a. The little child compared to the Pharisees
         b. The little child compared to His disciples
      3. Jesus made the deep things easy to understand
         a. He compared familiar things to spiritual
         b. A little child simply believes
      4. God said it; I believe it; that settles it
      5. Faith that cuts through religious ceremony and believes
      6. Faith that is not awed by titles or offices
      7. Faith that places no limits on the power and love of God
   B. *Faith That Rises to All the Challenges of Life (Heb. 11)*
      1. Faith is built on the conviction that God can do anything
      2. Faith made Abel worship God (Heb. 11:4)
      3. Faith made Enoch walk with God (Heb. 11:5)
      4. Faith made Noah work for God (Heb. 11:7)
      5. Faith made Abraham obey God (Heb. 11:8)
      6. Faith has sustained many in tough times
      7. Faith removes all limits on God's ability to provide
      8. Faith claims the resources of God in every crisis

137

   9. Heroic faith is the fruit of the Spirit
   10. "If thou canst believe, all things are possible" (Mark 9:23)

C. *Faith That Proves the Believer's Life Is Different (James 2:18)*
   1. Faith in the deepest and broadest sense
   2. Can be translated "fidelity"
   3. This is the carry through dimension to faith
   4. Produces visible evidence: faithfulness
      a. Faithful to Christ
      b. Faithful to His Word
      c. Faithful to His work in the local church
      d. Faithful in the use of talents and gifts
      e. Faithful in use of material resources

III. Conclusion
A. *Describe Your Faith*
   1. Is it childlike?
   2. Is it sufficient for life's challenges?
   3. Has it changed your life?
B. *Do You Need a Faith Lift?*
   1. Get back to the Bible (Rom. 10:17)
   2. Be filled with the Spirit (Eph. 5:19)
C. *Commit Your Life to the Lord and Watch Your Faith Grow*

The Fruit of the Spirit Is Meekness

Series on the Fruit of the Spirit   *Galatians 5:23*

I. Introduction
    A. *The Holy Spirit and the Believer*
        1. Enters the believer at conversion to Christ (1 Cor. 6:20)
        2. Baptizes the believer into the body of Christ (1 Cor. 12:13)
        3. Seals the believer to the day of redemption (Eph. 4:30)
    B. *The Fruit of the Spirit Is the Normal Christian Experience*
    C. *Meekness As the Fruit of the Spirit*
        1. Meekness is having a patient, gentle disposition
        2. Meekness is humble submissiveness to God's will
    D. *Examples of Meekness in the Bible*

II. Body
    A. *The Meek Learner (James 1:21)*
        1. Receiving God's Word with meekness
        2. Humility in receiving what God has to say to us
            a. The absence of pride
            b. The opposite of rebellion
        3. To receive God's Word one must take it in
            a. Calls for reading the Bible regularly and prayerfully
            b. Calls for hearing the Bible consistently
            c. Calls for listening with the heart
            d. Calls for shutting out less important messages
        4. Like little children learning new things
        5. Eager to do the will of God whatever the cost
        6. Total concentration on what God says to us
            a. Eliminating carnal input
            b. Welcoming Biblical truth
    B. *The Meek Leader (Num. 12:3)*
        1. Moses was the meekest man of all
            a. How surprising
            b. The man who would face Pharaoh
            c. The man who would deliver his people

   2. Have we been confused about what makes a
       leader?
       a. Leaders do not have to be dynamic
       b. Leaders do not have to be dictatorial
   3. Humility more important than impressive
       credentials
   4. Submission to God's will more important than
       public relations
   5. Has pride been keeping you from God's best?
   6. Watch for signs of meekness in yourself and others
C. *The Meek Lamb (Matt. 11:29)*
   1. "I am meek," said Jesus
   2. He was the Lamb of God (John 1:29)
       a. What could be more meek than a lamb?
       b. The lamb for the sacrifice
   3. He did not resist crucifixion (1 Peter 1:21–25)
   4. "Not my will but thine be done" (Luke 22:40)
   5. Jesus was the supreme example of meekness

III. Conclusion
   A. *Are You Always Demanding Your Own Way?*
       1. Do you have trouble getting along with others?
       2. Do you get angry when things don't go your way?
   B. *Ask the Holy Spirit for Meekness*
   C. *He Will Produce the Meekness of Jesus in You*

The Fruit of the Spirit Is Temperance (Self-Control)

Series on the Fruit of the Spirit Ends

*Galatians 5:23;
Philippians 4:13*

I. Introduction
   A. *Resolutions and Regrets*
      1. Good intentions often end in failure
      2. When areas of life are out of control
         a. "I'll never do that again"
         b. "I'm going to quit smoking, drinking, gaining weight"
         c. "I'm going to control my tongue"
   B. *The Holy Spirit Offers Self-Control*
      1. The fruit that delivers from despair
      2. The fruit that enables you to win
   C. *How to Gain Self-Control*

II. Body
   A. *Exchange Your Self-Confidence for Faith (Phil. 4:13)*
      1. "I can do all things"
      2. A plus and minus about self confidence
         a. Self-confidence enables us to achieve some things
         b. Self-confidence limits us to human potential
      3. The Holy Spirit adds a divine dimension
         a. Joshua leading his people to victory over Jericho
         b. Young David defeating mighty Goliath
         c. Unlearned disciples turning the world upside down
      4. Defeat can be changed to victory in God's power
         a. All the discipline we need is available from the Lord
         b. Discipline is self-control in action
         c. Discipline is the evidence of the Holy Spirit's power
      5. Trust God to enable you to do what you ought to do

   B. *Exchange Your Will Power for God's Power (Phil. 4:13)*
     1. "I can do all things through Christ"
       a. Trade your "I want to" for "I can"
       b. "You can" through the power of God
     2. You've been trying to win with will power
       a. Your will power is limited
       b. God's power is unlimited
       c. God's unlimited power is operative in you
       d. Yielding to the Holy Spirit provides self-control
     3. Every Christian is equipped to win

   C. *Exchange Your Weakness for God's Strength (Phil. 4:13)*
     1. "Strengtheneth me"
     2. Your strength is limited
       a. No wonder you have failed
       b. Good intentions weren't realized
     3. Back to God's unlimited power
       a. No resolve is beyond you
       b. No victory you can't win

III. Conclusion
   A. *Exchange Your Guilt for God's Forgiveness*
     1. Guilt over past failures brings depression
       a. We don't want to try again
       b. We begin to think like losers
     2. Guilt is real because all have sinned
     3. God forgives the guilty (1 John 1:9)
     4. God will make you a winner
   B. *The Fruit of the Spirit Will Change Your Life*
   C. *Give the Holy Spirit Full Control Today*

A Christian's Most Important Appointment

2 Corinthians 5:10

I. **Introduction**
   A. *An Age of Appointments*
      1. Appointments with doctors, dentists, mechanics
      2. Sometimes earthly appointments are cancelled
   B. *An Appointment Every Christian Must Keep*
      1. More important than any other appointment
      2. An appointment that will not be rescheduled
   C. *This Appointment Is the Judgment Seat of Christ*

II. **Body**
   A. *We Must Stand before the One Who Saved Us*
      1. An appointment only for believers
      2. Lost people not judged until later (Rev. 20:5)
      3. Not one Christian will be excused ("We must")
      4. Not one Christian will be left out ("all")
      5. Think of who we will be meeting
         a. The One who came down to save us
         b. The One who endured the cross for us
         c. The One who arose for us
         d. The One who has taken away our sins
         e. The One who has heard our prayers
      6. We ought to live with this meeting in mind
   B. *We Must Stand before the One Who Knows All about Us*
      1. "We must all appear" (be made manifest)
      2. Standing before the One who knows His sheep (John 10:27)
         a. Nothing will be hidden from Him
         b. No way to bluff our way through this meeting
      3. Some things Jesus knows about us
         a. What occupies our minds
         b. What we read at home and at work
         c. How we spend or give our money
         d. The degree of our dedication
         e. The secret desires of our hearts
      4. What adjustments ought you to make before that meeting?

        a.   What changes in priorities?
        b.   What changes in goals?

C. *We Must Stand Before the One Who Has Commissioned Us*
1. Each Christian has been commissioned to serve
   a. We are to be ambassadors for Christ (2 Cor. 5:20)
   b. We are to be witnesses for Christ (Acts. 1:8)
   c. We are to be His lights in a dark world (Phil. 2:15)
2. Rewards to be given at this appointment (Rev. 22:12)
   a. The Crown of Life for soul winning (1 Thess. 2:19)
   b. The Crown of Righteousness for loving His appearing (2 Tim. 4:8)
   c. The crown of life for suffering (James 1:12)
   d. The crown of glory for feeding God's people (1 Peter 5:4)
3. Rewards given affected by how we have lived
   a. What we have done in the body
   b. Whether good or bad

III. Conclusion
A. *The Judgment Seat of Christ Follows the Rapture of the Church*
B. *Signs of the Lord's Return Are Multiplying*
C. *Your Most Important Appointment Is Getting Closer Every Day*

Worry-Free Living

I. Introduction
- A. *A Text to Overcome Worry*
  1. A text for us all
  2. Who has escaped the temptation to fear?
  3. Worry is the opposite of faith
- B. *A Text That Is Easy to Understand*
  1. Speaks of food and clothing
  2. Speaks of birds and flowers
- C. *Steps to Worry Free Living*

II. Body
- A. *Look About You (vv. 25–31)*
  1. Take no thought for your life
     a. Stop worrying about survival
     b. Put away anxiety over daily provisions
  2. Has God not provided food and clothing in the past?
     a. How many times have you gone hungry?
     b. How many times have you been without clothing?
  3. God feeds the birds
     a. They do no sowing or reaping
     b. They never harvest and store up food
  4. God clothes the flowers
     a. They're not making petals
     b. God makes them beautiful every year
     c. They are clothed better than Solomon
  5. You are much more important than birds or flowers
  6. You are the object of God's love and attention
- B. *Look Above You (vv. 32–33)*
  1. "Your heavenly Father knows"
     a. What comfort in these words
     b. Nothing takes God by surprise
  2. While you've been worrying
     a. God has been working
     b. God has been aware and active

         3. Don't act like the faithless ones (v. 32)
            a. Worry spoils your testimony
            b. Others need to observe your faith
         4. The great faith and provision promise (6:33)
            a. Seek God first
            b. All else will be added to you
     C. *Live One Day at a Time (v. 34)*
         1. Stop being anxious about tomorrow
            a. Worrying doesn't provide strength for tomorrow
            b. Worrying just drains strength from today
         2. Tomorrow can be tough
         3. Can you feel safe for today?
         4. God will be alive tomorrow too

III. Conclusion
     A. *A Bible Plan for Worry-Free Living*
         1. Remember God loves you; the cross proves His love
         2. Refuse to carry tomorrow's burdens today
         3. Replace worry with positive thoughts and praise (Phil. 4:6–8)
     B. *Stop That Sinful Worrying*
     C. *Trust God to Demonstrate His Love*

Confessing Christ Publicly

Luke 12:8

I. Introduction

A. *Do You Consider Yourself a Secret Believer?*
   1. Why would anyone want to be silent about Jesus?
   2. Why not tell the world of the Savior?
   3. Joseph of Arimathaea broke his silence after the cross

B. *A Great Promise about Confessing Christ Openly*
   1. Confessing Christ before men brings rewards
   2. He will confess us before the angels

C. *Confessing Christ Publicly Is as Simple as A–B–C*

II. Body

A. *Confessing Christ by Acknowledging Him with Our Lips (Rom. 10:9)*
   1. "Confess with thy mouth"
   2. Talking about our newfound faith is normal
      a. We are to let others know we've been saved
      b. This often brings others to Christ
   3. "Let the redeemed of the LORD say so" (Ps. 107:2)
   4. Peter and John couldn't keep quiet about Christ (Acts 4:20)
   5. New converts are often the best evangelists
      a. Their joy convinces others to believe
      b. Explaining the change in them results in more converts
   6. We should never be ashamed to speak of Jesus

B. *Confessing Christ by Baptism (Matt. 28:18–20)*
   1. The importance of baptism in the Great Commission
   2. Baptism was public and important to the early church
      a. Three thousand converts baptized (Acts 2:41)
      b. Philip baptized his Ethiopian convert (Acts 8:36–40)
      c. Paul was baptized (Acts 9:18)
      d. Cornelius was baptized (Acts 10:47–48)
   3. Baptism is a picture of the Gospel

    4. Baptism is public identification with Jesus
      a. Identification with His death
      b. Identification with His burial
      c. Identification with His resurrection
    5. Have you been baptized?
    6. Your baptism may bring someone to Christ

C. *Confessing Christ by Consistency in Christian Living (2 Cor. 3:2)*
    1. Living epistles "known and read of all men"
      a. The world is looking for Christians who are real
      b. Others judge Christ by how we live
    2. "All Christians are either Bibles or libels" (F.B.Meyer)
    3. "When a man becomes a Christian even his dog and cat should know it" (Rowland Hill)
    4. Characteristics of Christ that should be confessed in us
      a. His love for people
      b. His compassion for those in pain or need
      c. His willingness to forgive
      d. His humility (Phil.2:5–7)

III. Conclusion
    A. *Have You Acknowledged Christ in Words Today?*
    B. *Have You Been Baptized Since You Believed?*
    C. *Are You Living a Consistent Christian Life?*
    D. *The Angels Are Interested*
    E. *Others Are Interested Too*

What New Doctrine Is This?

Acts 17:15–34

I. **Introduction**

   A. *Paul at Athens*

     1. The great literary center of the ancient world

     2. Paul sent for Silas and Timothy to join him (v. 15)

   B. *Paul Finds a City Given to Idolatry*

     1. "Easier to find a god than a man" (Greek Philosopher)

     2. "Practically every false deity worshiped on earth could be found in Athens" (Ironside)

   C. *Paul Presenting Christ to a Searching City*

II. **Body**

   A. *Christ the Fulfillment of the Intellectual Desire (vv. 17–21)*

     1. Paul in the synagogue and the market

     2. The philosophers challenge him

       a. What will this babbler say?

       b. They hoped he would tell them something new

     3. Athens the philosophic center of the world

       a. The Epicurians taught self expression

       b. The Stoics taught self repression

     4. Paul taught them of the cross and resurrection of Jesus

       a. Deep enough for philosophers to ponder

       b. Yet simple enough for a child to receive

     5. Christ was the intellectual's intellectual

       a. Asking and answering questions in the temple at twelve

       b. He spoke with authority and the people listened

       c. He needed no teachers concerning the mind of man

       d. He understood the nature of man (John 2:23–25)

   B. *Christ the Fulfillment of the Religious Desire (vv. 22–26)*

     1. "I perceive that you are very religious"

     2. Why man is religious by nature

       a. He was created to have fellowship with God

       b. He is a sinner and therefore feels guilty

       c.   The law of God is written in his heart
           (Rom. 2:14–15)

   3. Paul introduces "The unknown God"

   4. The unknown God can be known (2 Tim. 1:12)

       a.   Beyond the idols, altars, and images, a living God

       b.   Beyond the spires, temples, and prayer books, a living God

   5. We know God through faith in Christ (John 14:6)

   6. Trusting Christ fulfills the need to have fellowship with God

  C. *Christ the Fulfillment of the Emotional Desire (vv. 27–34)*

   1. Feeling after God to find Him

       a.   The only place "feel" is found in the New Testament

       b.   Without the Scriptures, man is on an emotional search

       c.   When we come to faith in Christ proper feelings follow

   2. Christ meets the emotional needs of those who come to Him

       a.   What emotion is deeper than love?

       b.   What emotion lifts one higher than joy?

       c.   What emotion is more satisfying than peace?

   3. Emotional satisfaction is fulfilled in Jesus

III. Conclusion

  A. *Unless the Intellectual Desire Ends in Christ It Ends in Pride*

  B. *Unless the Religious Desire Ends in Christ It Ends in Formalism*

  C. *Unless the Emotional Desire Ends in Christ It Ends in Fanaticism*

  D. *Jesus Is All We Need*

The Bible and the Battle

Matthew 4:1–11

I. Introduction
A. *Every Christian Is in a Spiritual War*
1. Our adversary is the Devil (1 Peter 5:8)
2. Salvation does not deliver us from this battle
3. It does equip us to win

B. *Temptation Is a Daily Part of This War*
1. This is hand-to-hand conflict
2. The Bible in the hand and heart assures victory

C. *How Jesus Used the Bible When Tempted*
1. Texts He used to overcome the enemy
2. How appropriate these were for the conflict!

II. Body
A. *Man Shall Not Live by Bread Alone (vv. 1–4)*
1. Jesus was hungry
   a. He had fasted forty days and nights
   b. The Tempter comes when we are weak
2. "Command that these stones be made bread"
   a. This was well within Christ's power
   b. Never follow Satan's suggestions
   c. Reject them even when they sound good
3. Jesus answers the Tempter with Scripture (v. 4; Deut. 8:3)
   a. We need more than bread in this battle
   b. God's Word is to be our daily food
4. We can defeat Satan with Scripture
5. The Word of God is the sword of the Spirit (Eph. 6:17)
6. The Bible must become our daily bread

B. *Thou Shalt Not Tempt the Lord Thy God (v. 7)*
1. Tempted on the pinnacle of the temple
   a. Many temptations come in religious places
   b. We are most vulnerable when in high places
2. Satan now begins to quote Scripture (Ps. 91:11–12)
   a. Cultists often quote Scripture
   b. Satan as an angel of light (2 Cor. 11:13–15)
3. The Scripture Jesus quoted in overcoming this temptation

151

        a. Thou shalt not tempt the Lord thy God
           (v. 7; Deut 6:16)
        b. Some things that tempt God
           (1) Complaining about His provision
               (Exod. 7:7)
           (2) Not trusting God to keep His promises
               (Num. 14:22)
           (3) Doubting God's power (Ps. 78:41)
           (4) Hardening our hearts when He speaks
               (Heb. 3:9)
    4. Have you been tempting God?

C. *Thou Shalt Worship the Lord Thy God (v. 10)*
    1. Satan offers the world if Jesus will worship him
    2. "Get thee hence, Satan"
        a. The first time this precedes "It is written"
        b. Worshiping Satan is reprehensible to Christ
    3. Many worship people and things rather than the
       Lord
    4. The Lord should have all of our worship and
       service
        a. Who do you worship?
        b. Who do you serve?

III. Conclusion
  A. *Are You Struggling with Temptation?*
  B. *Take the Bible into Battle*
  C. *The Sword of the Spirit Will Bring Victory Every Time*

Desires of the Disciples

John 13:36–14:9

I. Introduction

    A. *Jesus Prepares His Disciples for His Coming Death*

        1. Difficult days are ahead for them

        2. Important instructions will be given

    B. *The Disciples Have Some Personal Questions and Desires*

        1. Peter wants to follow Jesus . . . now

        2. Thomas wants to know the way to heaven

        3. Philip wants to see the Father

    C. *How Jesus Answered Them All*

II. Body

    A. *The Desire of Peter to Follow Jesus . . . Now (13:37)*

        1. "Why cannot I follow thee now?"

        2. Jesus had already told Peter he could not follow him then

            a. "Whither I go, thou canst not follow me now" (v. 36)

            b. He would be able to follow Jesus later

        3. Peter was trying to force God's plan into his timetable

            a. Nothing wrong with Peter's dedication

            b. Nothing wrong with his basic desire

            c. It was not God's time

        4. Many have tried to do the will of God on their terms

            a. This is sure to bring failure

            b. God's way and time are always best

    B. *The Desire of Thomas to Know the Way to Heaven (14:5)*

        1. "How can we know the way"

        2. Thomas had just heard the most loved text on heaven

            a. Jesus was going away to prepare mansions

            b. He would prepare special places for them

            c. He would come again and receive them to Himself

   3. Thomas wanted to make sure he would be included
      a. He wanted time in those mansions
      b. He was willing to do anything to get there
   4. He lacked assurance of heaven
      a. He should have been sure of heaven
      b. Jesus said, "and the way ye know"
      c. Those who know Jesus know the way to heaven
   5. Jesus settles it for Thomas: "I am the way, . . ." (v. 6)
      a. The way: that the will of man may choose it
      b. The truth: that the mind of man may comprehend it
      c. The life: that the heart of man may experience it
C. *The Desire of Philip to See the Father (14:8)*
   1. "Lord, show us the Father and it sufficeth us."
      a. Let us see the Father and we'll be satisfied
      b. It seems like a reasonable request
      c. But it reveals that Philip hadn't been listening
   2. "He that hath seen me hath the seen Father"
   3. The mystery of the Trinity
      a. To know about the Holy Spirit, listen to Jesus
      b. To know about Jesus, listen to the Holy Spirit
      c. To know about the Father, observe Jesus

III. **Conclusion**
   A. *What Are Your Desires?*
   B. *Are They Similar to Those of the Disciples?*
   C. *The Soul's Greatest Desires Are All Fulfilled in Jesus*

The Lord and Lydia

Acts 16:9–15

I. Introduction
   A. *The Macedonian Call (v. 9)*
      1. Paul's vision: "Come over into Macedonia and help us"
      2. Expectations high over the prospects of converts
   B. *On to Philippi*
      1. Philippi was a Roman colony
      2. After a number of days nothing worth recording
      3. Sometimes we become disappointed too quickly
   C. *Down by the Riverside*
      1. The prayer meeting by the river
      2. A Jewish meeting; it was on the Sabbath
         a. Like many prayer meetings today, all women
         b. They ministered to the women
      3. Lydia, a Gentile at a Jewish prayer meeting

II. Body
   A. *Lydia Found Her Need So Great She Found Someplace to Go (v. 14)*
      1. Lydia was a businesswoman
         a. A seller of purple from Thyatira
         b. Paul had been forbidden to go to Asia (v. 7)
         c. God brought an Asian to Paul
      2. Lydia had come to the meeting to worship God
         a. Sick of idolatry and emptiness
         b. Seeking the Lord
         c. Those who seek the Lord find Him (Jer. 29:13)
      3. The Lord opened Lydia's heart to Paul's message
      4. Is your heart open to the message of Christ?
   B. *Lydia Found Salvation So Great She Wanted Others to Know (v. 15)*
      1. She was baptized
         a. Members of her household also believed and were baptized
         b. We don't know how many family members or employees
      2. Lydia wanted to confess Christ publicly

        a.   How this must have affected those who witnessed it

        b.   Evidently a number of others received Christ (v. 40)

    3.   Why Lydia wanted others to know

        a.   She had found life's greatest possession

        b.   She wanted to share the good news

C. *Lydia Found Her Blessing So Great She Let Her Joy Overflow (v. 15)*

    1.   "Come into my house"

    2.   Her joy made her hospitable

        a.   Invited Paul and the others to her house

        b.   She hoped they saw evidence of her faith

        c.   She invited them to stay as long as possible (abide)

        d.   She urged them to accept her invitation

    3.   She already loved the fellowship of other believers

    4.   She gave good evidence of her faith in Christ

III. Conclusion

A. *Lydia, an Asian, Was the First Convert in Europe*

    1.   God's plan to reach the world is through people

    2.   Now the Gospel would go to both Europe and Asia

B. *God Had Been at Work in Lydia's Life Before This Meeting*

    1.   Has God been speaking to you about salvation?

    2.   Is this the reason you are present?

C. *Allow the Lord to Open Your Heart to His Word*

Staying Positive in a Negative World

Philippians 4:6–9

I. Introduction

A. *We Live in a Negative World (John 16:33)*
1. This negative world has many problems
2. We are affected by the world's trouble
   a. Violence, war, crime
   b. Alcohol, abortion, home breakups
   c. Hospitals, cemeteries, prisons

B. *We Are Not to Be Negative People*
1. We are to be rejoicing people (Phil. 3:1)
2. We are to focus on positive thoughts and praise
   a. Things true, honest, just
   b. Things pure, lovely, of good report
   c. "If there be any virtue . . . any praise"
3. Still, sometimes Christians are negative . . . complaining

C. *How Can We Stay Positive in This Negative World?*

II. Body

A. *We Must Respond to God's Love (vv. 6–7)*
1. God loves us in spite of the circumstances
2. God's love is shown in creation
3. God's love is revealed in the Bible
4. God's love is most clearly seen at the cross
5. God's love is demonstrated through answered prayer

B. *We Must Reprogram Our Thinking (v. 8)*
1. We are constantly bombarded by negative messages
2. The downside of the age of instant communication
   a. Aware of the world's problems continually
   b. All violent acts reported to us immediately
3. Psychological dangers of constant negative input
4. Physical dangers of constant negative input
5. The importance of faith-building input
   a. Developing a devotional life
   b. Daily Bible reading and prayer
   c. Starting every day thankful
   d. Expecting God to come through

157

C. *We Must Recognize the Best in Others (v. 8)*
1. All people are imperfect
   a. No perfect people or churches
   c. No perfect pastors
2. People do have many positive things about them
   a. Some are true, honest, and just
   b. Some are well reported of by friends
   c. Some do praiseworthy things
3. "I thank my God upon every remembrance of you" (Phil. 1:3)
   a. How could Paul say this?
   b. He chose to remember the positive things about them
D. *We Must Reach Out to Lost and Hurting People (v. 9)*
1. Let's look on the fields rather than the faults of others
2. Paul's plea for the Philippians to do as he was doing
   a. Paul was always reaching out to the lost
   b. He loved souls and longed for their salvation
3. Winning people to Christ brings positive joy (Ps. 126:6)

III. **Conclusion**
A. *Faith in Christ Enables Us to Be Positive in This Negative World*
B. *A Positive Testimony Will Bring Others to Our Savior*

What It Means to Be Lost

Luke 19:10; Ephesians 2:12; John 3:26

I. **Introduction**
   A. *"Lost" Is a Lost Word in Many Churches*
      1. Most preaching and teaching on other subjects
      2. Subjects more popular and pleasant have priority
   B. *The Lost Word Keeps Many Lost*
      1. People need to know the consequences of sin
      2. People need to know how serious it is to be lost
      3. Jesus came to seek and save the lost (Luke 19:10)
   C. *What Does It Mean to Be Lost?*

II. **Body**
   A. *To Be Lost Is to Be Without Hope (Eph. 2:12)*
      1. "Having no hope"
      2. Hope has to do with assurance of salvation
         a. "The hope which is laid up for you in heaven" (Col. 1:5)
         b. "Christ in you the hope of glory" (Col. 1:27)
         c. "Which hope we have as an anchor of the soul" (Heb. 6:19)
         d. A hope that is steadfast and sure (Heb. 6:19)
      3. Lost people have no prospect of heaven
         a. When loved ones die they borrow Christian hope
         b. They talk of seeing loved ones again but can't be sure
      4. To be lost is to be hopeless
   B. *To Be Lost Is to Be Without God in the World (Eph. 2:12)*
      1. "Without God in the world"
      2. Paul reminds the Ephesian believers of their past
         a. They had once been without hope
         b. They had once been without God in the world
      3. Times when people desperately need God
         a. When in deep emotional distress
         b. When threatened with financial ruin
         c. When facing serious surgery or other illness
         d. When family problems bring them to despair

159

      4. Christians flee to their Lord in such times
      5. Lost people have nowhere to go
         a. Peter's question: "Lord, to whom shall we go?" (John 6:68)
         b. How sad to be alone in times of trouble!

  C. *To Be Lost Is to Be Without Eternal Life (1 John 5:12)*
      1. "He that hath not the Son of God hath not life"
      2. Life here is short at its longest
         a. We live only an average of 70–80 years
         b. Medical science still can't extend life very long
      3. Jesus offers eternal life (John 3:16; 5:24)
         a. Who can fathom eternity?
         b. "No less days to sing God's praise than when we'd first begun" (John Newton)
      4. Do you have assurance of eternal life?

III. Conclusion

  A. *We Are All Sinners (Rom. 6:23)*
  B. *Not One More Sin Is Needed to Be Lost Forever*
  C. *Christ Died for Sinners (Rom. 5:8)*
  D. *What Sinners Receive When They Come to Christ for Salvation*
      1. They receive hope (assurance of salvation)
      2. They receive fellowship with God
      3. They receive eternal life
  E. *Why Not Come to Him Now?*

The Power of Positive Action

Colossians 3:23

I. **Introduction**
   A. *Paul the Emotionally Mature Man*
      1. Rejoicing in the Lord always (Phil 4:4)
      2. Experiencing peace that passes understanding (Phil. 4:7)
      3. Content in any situation (Phil. 4:11)
   B. *Paul a Man of Action*
      1. Not huddling in a corner afraid to advance
      2. Not trembling about the future; too much to do today
      3. Not in despair; too much living to do
      4. Not holding back; too many to win to Christ
   C. *Do Something for Christ That Stretches You*

II. **Body**
   A. *Do Something to Enrich Your Christian Life*
      1. Get serious about Bible study
      2. Start memorizing Bible verses
      3. Make a list of your blessings and give thanks
      4. Read a Christian book
      5. Put away all bitterness and anger: forgive everyone
   B. *Do Something for Your Family*
      1. Ask your wife or husband to forgive you for being cross
      2. Express appreciation for what loved ones do for you
      3. Hug your children and tell them you love them
      4. Help family members develop their talents
      5. Call your parents and thank them for love and prayers
      6. Stop griping and start giving compliments
      7. Start having daily devotions with your family
   C. *Do Something for Your Church*
      1. Write an appreciation note to your pastor
      2. Volunteer to teach a Sunday school class
      3. Offer to use your car to bring people to church
      4. Visit absentees and report the results to your pastor

      5.   Increase your giving

      6.   Refuse to take part in gossip or criticism of leaders

      7.   Join the choir or use some other talent you've been hiding

      8.   Start a prayer group for revival

  D. *Do Something to Fulfill Your Responsibility to World Evangelism*

      1.   Contact neighborhood families and invite them to church

      2.   Visit a lonely person who needs Christ

      3.   Start giving out tracts every day

      4.   Write to a missionary and enclose a gift

      5.   Take a class on how to do personal witnessing

      6.   Increase your giving to missions

      7.   Pray for the special needs of missionaries

III. Conclusion

  A. *Let's Stop Being Part-Time Christians*

      1.   We are to serve the Lord heartily

      2.   No such thing as sacred and secular things for Christians

      3.   Everything we do should be done for the Lord

  B. *"Like a Mighty Army Moves the Church of God"*

      1.   Too often this isn't true

      2.   Let it start being true in you and me

      3.   We may have come to the kingdom for such a time as this

Faith That Does Not Save

James 2:14–26

I. Introduction

  A. *We Are Saved by Faith (Eph. 2:8; Rom. 5:1)*
1. No one can be saved by good works (Eph. 2:9)
2. No one can be saved by keeping the law (Gal. 2:16)
3. No one can be saved apart from faith in Christ (John 14:6)

  B. *Startling Statements by James about Salvation by Faith*
1. Seeming contradictions to Paul
2. Really in full agreement with Paul (Rom. 10:9–10)

  C. *What Is This Faith James Says Does Not Save?*

II. Body

  A. *Faith That Is Mere Profession Does Not Save (vv. 14–17)*
1. "If a man say that he hath faith and hath not works"
   a. Emphasis on "say"
   b. This is profession without evidence of salvation
2. This professor of faith shows no fruit of faith
   a. His professed faith produces no works
   b. Like speaking kindly to the hungry but not feeding them
3. Paul agrees: Faith in Christ makes us different (2 Cor. 5:17)
   a. Salvation causes old things to pass away
   b. All things become new to those who are born again

  B. *Faith That Does Not Bring Spiritual Life Does Not Save (vv. 17–18)*
1. "Faith, if it hath not works, is dead"
2. This faith is a counterfeit
   a. It is not childlike trust in Christ
   b. It is not trusting Christ alone
   c. It is called faith but is not faith
   d. It is some religious act or experience called faith

    3. Faith in Christ always brings new life
        (John 3:3–5, 16)
        a. There are no exceptions
        b. Jesus turns no one away (John 6:37)
        c. This invitation is for the "whosoevers"
            (Rom. 10:13)
  C. *Faith That Is Merely Intellectual Agreement Does Not
     Save (v. 19)*
     1. Believing the facts is not necessarily faith
         a. Demons believe there is one God
         b. They tremble when they think about it
         c. Their acceptance of the facts does not help
             them
     2. One can agree with the facts of the Gospel and be
         lost
     3. Intellectual assent is not really faith
         a. It is like "another gospel" in Galatians
             (Gal. 1:6)
         b. Paul says it was just called the Gospel
             (Gal. 1:7)
     4. One must move from facts to faith to be saved

III. **Conclusion**
  A. *Examples of Living Faith (vv. 21–25)*
     1. Abraham trusted God and it moved him to
         obedience
     2. His faith produced works
     3. He became known as the friend of God
     4. Rahab's faith caused her to save the Israeli spies
  B. *One Who Places Faith in Christ As Savior Has Living
     Faith*
     1. It is not mere profession
     2. It is not counterfeit
  C. *This Is Biblical Faith*
     1. Do not think it difficult to achieve
     2. It is a sinner's response to God's love shown at the
         cross
     3. It is trusting Jesus with the faith of a child

The Biggest Liar in Town

John 8:44; John 10:10

I. **Introduction**
   A. *Questions and Answers About the Devil*
      1. Is Satan a real personality or just an evil force?
         a. Should we remove the "d" from devil?
         b. The Bible says he is a personality
            (Matt. 4:1; Rev. 20:2)
      2. Is the devil now in hell?
         a. No, but that will be his future place
            (Rev. 20:10)
         b. Now he is actively tempting and destroying
            (1 Peter 5:8)
   B. *What's the Devil Like?*

II. **Body**
   A. *He Is a Murderer (John 8:44)*
      1. "He was a murderer from the beginning"
      2. Satan the murderer, and sin (Rom. 6:23)
         a. God's warning about the forbidden fruit: death
            (Gen. 3:3)
         b. Satan convinced Adam and Eve they wouldn't
            die (v. 4)
         c. In their disobedience death came to us all
            (Rom. 5:12)
      3. Satan delights in man's destruction
      4. God delights in man's salvation
      5. Satan the murderer, and society
         a. Tempts people to murder through envy (Cain)
         b. Tempts people to murder through lust (Herod)
         c. Tempts people to murder through greed
            (Ahab)
      6. Satan the murderer, and the destruction of self
         a. Judas after the betrayal of Jesus
         b. Tempts people to suicide because of despair
         c. Tempts people to suicide because of feeling
            unloved
   B. *He Is a Liar (John 8:44)*
      1. "He is a liar, and the father of it"

165

    2. The father of falsehoods
       a. The first recorded lie "Ye shall not surely die"
       b. Death has flowed from that lie through the centuries
    3. Some lies to expect from the biggest liar in town
       a. Promises freedom and gives bondage
       b. Promises good times and gives grief
       c. Promises fun and gives frustration
       d. Promises merriment and gives misery
    4. Satan lies to young and old
       a. He delights to ruin a life in youth
       b. We're never too old to be tempted

C. *He Is a Thief (John 10:10)*
    1. "To steal, and kill, and destroy"
    2. Thieves and the *thief*
       a. Many false Christs before Jesus came, and after
       b. Their purpose to steal, kill, and destroy the sheep
       c. Satan is the *thief*: the one behind them all
    3. Satan tried to steal the throne of God (Isa. 14:12–14)
    4. Satan tries to steal the place of God in our lives
    5. Satan tries to steal the rightful worship of God (Matt. 4:9)

III. Conclusion

A. *How to Overcome the Biggest Liar in Town*
    1. Submit yourself to God and resist the Devil
    2. James says "He will flee from you" (James 4:7)

B. *We Overcome the Liar Through the One Who Is the Truth*

C. *Christ Provides Victory over Satan Every Time*

The Devil in His Best Dress-Suit

2 Corinthians 11:13–15

I. Introduction
A. *Misconceptions About the Devil*
1. Cartoon characterizations are untrue
2. The devil is not now in hell
B. *The Rise of Satanic Religions in the Last Days (1 Tim. 4:1)*
1. People involved with seducing spirits
2. People accepting doctrines of demons
C. *The Devil Is More Dangerous When Clothed with Respectability*
1. How can we recognize our enemy when he is in disguise?
2. What is the Devil doing when in his best dress-suit?

II. Body
A. *He Is Trying to Complicate the Gospel (v. 13)*
1. The wonderful simple Gospel message (1 Cor. 15:3–4)
   a. Christ died for our sins according to the Scriptures
   b. He was buried and rose again according to the Scriptures
2. We are saved by faith alone (John 3:16)
3. False teachers add works or law-keeping to grace
   a. This happened to the Galatians (Gal. 3:1–3)
   b. Paul pointed out the error of this teaching (Gal. 2:21)
4. The Devil's arguments sound so convincing
   a. Sound like a higher standard of holiness
   b. He ridicules being saved by grace through faith
5. Adding to the Gospel is taking away from it
   a. To add anything to faith reduces faith's power
   b. Adding works or legalism subtracts from grace
6. Hold to the simplicity that is in Christ (2 Cor. 11:3)
B. *He Is Contradicting the Message of the Cross (v. 14)*
1. The Devil hates the message of the cross

167

2. Satan temporarily deceived Peter about the cross (Matt. 16:23)
   a. "Be it far from thee, Lord" (Matt. 16:22)
   b. "Get thee behind me, Satan" (Matt. 16:23)
3. There are only two religions
   a. Satan's religion says, "Do this and live"
   b. Christ says, "It's done; believe and live"
4. Rejecting the cross appeals to some
   a. The cross seems too violent, too bloody
   b. Some hymnals no longer contain songs about the blood
   c. Only the way of the cross leads home

C. *He Is Causing Controversy Among Christians (2 Cor. 11:15)*
   1. Satan's workers appear to be righteous
      a. Many who cause trouble in churches sound so right
      b. Bitterness and strife are from the Devil (James 3:14–16)
   2. The devil tries to divide and conquer
   3. Troublemakers often appear to be super spiritual
   4. When Christians forgive one another the Devil is defeated
      a. Forgiveness would revive most churches
      b. Putting away strife pleases the Lord (James 3:17–18)

III. Conclusion

A. *Recognize the Devil When He Comes Appearing Respectable*
   1. Resist him when he appears in his best dress-suit
   2. Take him to the cross where he was defeated by Jesus

B. *Christ Will Someday Expose the Devil for What He Really Is*

C. *Rejoice! We Are Going to Heaven and the Devil Is Going to Hell*

Handling End-Time Pressures

Luke 21:25–26; John 14

I. Introduction
A. *Christ Who Died and Rose Again Will Come Again*
   1. Many Scriptures describe conditions before His return
   2. Our text reveals some difficult days ahead
B. *The Triple Terror of the Last Days and How to Handle Them*
   1. Distress, perplexity, and fear will be epidemic
   2. The Holy Spirit equips believers to triumph over them

II. Body
A. *When We Are Distressed the Holy Spirit Gives Comfort (John 14:16)*
   1. "Distress of nations" (v. 25)
   2. Definition of distress: "An afflicted, wretched or exhausted condition; a state of extreme need"
   3. Our greatest need in distress is comfort
   4. The Holy Spirit is our comforter
   5. In this world we have trouble (John 16:33)
      a. We go through things we didn't think we would
      b. We go through things we didn't think we could
   6. We never experience trouble alone
      a. The Holy Spirit lives within the believer's body
      b. Our Comforter is always with us
   7. When we need comfort
      a. When we lose loved ones in death
      b. When others turn against us
      c. When events seem out of control
   8. The Holy Spirit replaces distress with peace
   9. The Comforter will never let us down
B. *When We Are Perplexed the Holy Spirit Gives Counsel (John 14:26)*
   1. Perplexed: "finding no way out"
      a. Do you feel trapped by your problems?
      b. You need the direction of the Lord

169

    2. When Jesus was with His disciples He taught them

    3. After the departure of Jesus the Holy Spirit taught them
        a. He enabled them to remember
        b. He guided them into all truth
        c. He taught them what to say

    4. The Holy Spirit does this for Christians today
        a. He will guide you through this perplexing time
        b. He knew it was coming and knows the way out of it

C. *When We Are Fearful the Holy Spirit Imparts Faith (John 14:27)*

    1. "Men's hearts failing them for fear" (v. 25)

    2. When we are afraid we need increased faith
        a. Fear and faith are opposites
        b. As faith increases fear decreases

    3. How the Holy Spirit imparts faith
        a. Through the Bible
        b. Through experience
        c. Through answered prayer

    4. "Let not your heart be troubled, neither let it be afraid"

III. Conclusion

A. *Stop Quenching the Holy Spirit (1 Thess. 5:19)*

    1. Accept His comfort when you are distressed

    2. Accept his counsel when you are perplexed

    3. Accept his peace when you are afraid

B. *These Difficult Times Are Signs That Our Lord Will Soon Return*

Earthquake-Proof Your Life

Psalm 46

I. **Introduction**
   A. *A Psalm for Times When Your World Is Shaking*
      1. There are many shaking times in life
      2. Perhaps you have been shaken by some recent experience
      3. Here is a Psalm to bring peace to your troubled heart
   B. *The Setting of This Comforting Psalm*
      1. Written during a foreign invasion of Israel
      2. Ideal for those who are targets of the enemy
   C. *What the Psalm Offers for Our Trembling Times*

II. **Body**
   A. *God's Presence (v. 1)*
      1. God appears at the beginning of the Psalm
         a. Not some impersonal supreme being
         b. This is the God who loves us
      2. The secret of peace is a personal relationship with God
         a. "God is our refuge"
         b. Like Psalm 23: "The Lord is my shepherd"
      3. "Our refuge" (hiding place)
         a. We hide in God when storms come
         b. We are safe with Him when our world is shaking
      4. "Our strength"
         a. God gives strength to those who are weak
         b. Waiting on the Lord renews our strength (Isa. 40:31)
      5. A very present help in trouble
         a. Our Lord is always with us
         b. He is greater than any trouble we face
   B. *God's Peace (vv. 2–7)*
      1. "Therefore we will not fear"
         a. Faith emerges and soars
         b. When faith comes fears flee
         c. Is your faith in the One who calmed the sea?

    2.   No fear though the earth be removed (v. 2)

    3.   No fear though the mountains fall into the sea (v. 2)

    4.   No fear though waves rage on the seas (v. 3)

    5.   No fear though earthquakes shake the mountains (v. 3)

    6.   Peace multiplies here as we look toward heaven
- a.   The river of life is there
- b.   The city of God is there
- c.   Jesus is preparing places there (John 14:1–3)

    7.   Meanwhile, the Lord of hosts is with us

C. *God's Promises (vv. 8–11)*

    1.   God is at work even when our world is shaking (Rom. 8:28)

    2.   God makes wars cease
- a.   He makes weapons worthless
- b.   Spurgeon: "The destroyers He destroys"

    3.   We can be still and leave the future with God
- a.   He has saved us through faith in Christ (Rom. 5:1)
- b.   We are part of His loving family (John 1:12–13)

III. Conclusion

A. *The Psalm Begins and Ends with God*

    1.   What a wonderful comfort for times of trouble

    2.   We begin and end each day in God's presence

B. *God Is Sufficient When Our World Is Shaking*

C. *We Can Trust Him to Bring Us Safely Through*

Time for Communion

1 Corinthians 11:23–34

I. **Introduction**
   A. *Differences in Frequency of Communion*
      1. Some have communion weekly, monthly, quarterly, etc.
      2. The Bible makes no time requirements for communion
   B. *Differences in Details of Communion Services*
      1. Some churches restrict communion to members
      2. Some invite all believers to take communion
      3. Some go to the altar; some are served in pews
   C. *Communion Does Not Save: Only Faith in Christ Saves*
   D. *What Then Are the Purposes of Communion?*

II. **Body**
   A. *A Time to Remember the Suffering and Death of Christ (vv. 24–25)*
      1. "This do in remembrance of me"
         a. Applies to both the bread and cup
         b. Symbols of His body and blood
      2. How much the cross must mean to the Lord
         a. Old Testament sacrifices looked forward to it (John 1:29)
         b. Heaven sings about it (Rev. 5:9)
         c. Communion reminds us of it
      3. Why so important to remember Christ's sufferings?
         a. It reminds us of the seriousness of sin
         b. It reminds us of God's love and grace
         c. It reminds us we have been forgiven
   B. *A Time to Look Forward to the Second Coming of Christ (v. 26)*
      1. "Till he come"
      2. Communion reminds us of His cross and His coming
      3. Communion reminds us of His groaning and His glory

173

    4. Each Communion service brings us nearer Christ's return
   - a. This should be a purifying experience (1 John 3:3)
   - b. Looking back to the price paid for our sins
   - c. Looking forward to the return of our sinless Savior

    5. Christ may return while some church is having Communion
   - a. Would you be ready if He returned today?
   - b. Would you feel confident or ashamed (1 John 2:28)?

C. *A Time for Self-Examination and Confession of Sins (vv. 28–31)*
   1. "But let a man examine himself"
      - a. In the light of the cross
      - b. In the light of Christ's return
   2. It is dangerous to be careless about Communion (1 Cor. 11:30)
      - a. Some had been stricken with illness
      - b. Some had died because of this
   3. Self examination and confession of sin prevents chastening
      - a. Self judgment prevents God's judgment (v. 31)
      - b. Confession of sin brings forgiveness (1 John 1:9)
   4. This is proper preparation for Communion

III. Conclusion

A. *Communion Should Keep Our Vision of the Cross Clear*

B. *Communion Should Keep Our Expectation of Christ's Return Fresh*

C. *Communion Should Keep Our Hearts Sensitive to Personal Sins*

D. *Are You Ready for Communion?*

Peace with God

Romans 5:1–6

I. **Introduction**
   A. *Peace: A Very Precious Possession*
      1. "We have peace with God through our Lord Jesus Christ"
      2. A pivotal verse in this important book
         a. Up to this point: sin, conviction, conclusions
         b. After this point: service, sacrifice, sanctification
   B. *The World Is Engaged in a Search for Personal Peace*
   C. *Peace with God Is the Most Important Peace of All*
      1. How do we get it?
      2. What will it do for us in the future?
      3. What will it do for us now?

II. **Body**
   A. *Peace with God Is Ours Through Faith in Jesus Christ (v. 1)*
      1. What a hard lesson for us to learn!
      2. Some things that do not bring peace with God
         a. Sorrow for sins
         b. Walking down a church aisle
         c. Keeping the Ten Commandments
         d. Prayer
      3. Peace with God comes only through faith in Christ
         a. Who can have it? Sinners
         b. When can they have it? When justified
         c. How can they be justified? By faith
         d. Faith in whom? Our Lord Jesus Christ
   B. *Peace with God Gives an Anticipation of Eternity (v. 2)*
      1. "And rejoice in hope of the glory of God"
      2. Without peace with God we do not look forward to eternity
         a. Ahead lies hell and judgment
         b. Every step leads us closer to them
         c. Every heartbeat moves us nearer pain, suffering, and hell

      3. Without peace with God we are not prepared to die
         a. We are not prepared to live until prepared to die
         b. We cannot be at peace until we are sure of heaven
         c. We cannot be sure of heaven until we have peace with God
      4. Peace with God enables us to look forward to the future
         a. We can think about the mansions prepared for us
         b. We can look forward to meeting loved ones
         c. We can anticipate being with Jesus

  C. *Peace with God Gives an Understanding of Life (vv. 3–5)*
      1. "Tribulation worketh patience"
      2. We begin to see a design in our difficulties
         a. Trouble makes us patient
         b. Patience contributes to experience
         c. Experience brings us hope
         d. Hope doesn't disappoint us
      3. The Holy Spirit fills our hearts with God's love
      4. This love helps us be confident, even in trials

III. Conclusion

  A. *God Invites You to Be at Peace with Him*
  B. *Christ Died for Us So That We Can Have This Peace (v. 6)*
  C. *Will You Receive Christ by Faith and Be at Peace with God?*

Looking Like Winners

Hebrews 12:1–2

I. Introduction
   A. *Three Thrilling Faith Chapters*
      1. We are saved by faith (ch. 10)
      2. These lived the life of faith (ch. 11)
      3. Here's how to live the life of faith (ch. 12)
   B. *Competing in Faith's Olympics*
      1. The most important race of all
      2. How can we win the race?

II. Body
   A. *We Must Look Around Us (v. 1)*
      1. We are all in a great arena
         a. Many are watching the race
         b. All eyes are on the runners
      2. Godly people have always been under scrutiny
         a. Noah was watched as he built the ark and preached
         b. Abraham was watched when headed for Canaan
         c. Moses was watched as he approached Pharaoh
      3. We are also watched to see how we run the race of faith
         a. A "great cloud of witnesses" brings great responsibility
         b. Many are counting on us to run well
         c. Some will enter the faith race because of how we run
         d. Some may choose not to run at all
      4. Have you looked like a winner to the witnesses today?
   B. *We Must Look Within Us (v. 1)*
      1. A winner prepares to win
         a. Winning is no accident
         b. Winners take steps that lead to victory
      2. Runners are slowed by weight
         a. Winners don't run in heavy clothes
         b. Winners don't carry anything to slow them down

    3. What's slowing you down in the Christian race?
       a. Lay aside anything that dulls your interest in God
       b. Lay aside anything that keeps you from the Bible
       c. Lay aside anything that harms your testimony
       d. Lay aside anything that keeps you out of church
    4. Weights aren't worth the risk of losing the race

C. *We Must Look to Jesus (v. 2)*
    1. "Looking unto Jesus"
       a. Three words for winners
       b. Others may let us down
       c. Jesus never fails
    2. Why look to Jesus?
       a. For encouragement (v. 3)
       b. For consistency (13:8)
       c. As our example (1 Peter 2:21)
    3. Jesus is the author and finisher of our faith
       a. Winners always start and end well
       b. Winners give their all throughout the race

III. Conclusion

    A. *The Race of Faith Calls for Great Endurance*
    B. *Joy Awaits Winners at the End of the Race*

The Lord Trains His Children

Hebrews 12:5–13

I. Introduction
    A. *"Chastening" Frightens Many*
        1. Brings visions of a sword ready to fall
        2. The word means "child training"
    B. *The Family of God*
        1. Being born again brings us into God's family
        2. Our loving Father is not an executioner
        3. His chastening is always for our good

II. Body
    A. *Who God Chastens (vv. 5–6)*
        1. The Lord chastens those He loves
        2. He chastens His dear children
            a. Lost people are not chastened
            b. Lost people face judgment and hell
        3. Some believers God chastened in the past
            a. God chastened Jonah for disobedience
            b. God chastened David for his sin with Bathsheba
            c. God chastened Israel for unbelief
        4. We cannot sin and win
            a. Christians cannot sin and get away with it
            b. Fathers who do not chasten are negligent
            c. God is not negligent with His children
    B. *Why God Chastens (v. 7–8)*
        1. God chastens because He loves us
        2. Chastening is evidence of being a child of God
        3. No chastening can mean we are not saved (v. 8)
        4. Earthly fathers chasten their children
            a. They do not chasten the children of others
            b. Chastening is a privilege reserved for God's children
        5. Other benefits of being a child of God
            a. We are part of God's family
            b. We are heirs of God; joint heirs with Christ (Rom. 8:17)
            c. We are citizens of heaven (Phil. 3:20)
            d. We have everlasting life (John 5:24)

6. God is training us for fruitful service for Him

C. *Results and Reactions to God's Chastening (vv. 9–13)*
   1. Reactions:
      a. We may not like it
      b. We may find it temporarily painful
      c. We should remember chastening is for our good
   2. Results:
      a. We become partakers of God's holiness
      b. We experience the peaceable fruit of righteousness
   3. These benefits come to those who learn from chastening

III. Conclusion

A. *Have You Ever Experienced God's Chastening?*
   1. Did you learn from it?
   2. Have you profited from it?
   3. Can you thank God for it?

B. *Are You Now Being Chastened?*
   1. Don't let your chastening be in vain
   2. Get back to serving God again (v. 13)

Why Christians Have Trials

Faith Under Fire Series Begins   *1 Peter 1:6–9*

I. **Introduction**
   A. *Peter Praises the Lord*
      1. His living hope (v. 3)
      2. His lasting inheritance (v. 4)
      3. His longing for final rewards (v. 6)
   B. *Now on a More Sober Note*
      1. Peter warns there may be tough times ahead
      2. He wants his readers to be prepared for them
   C. *What Can We Learn from Peter's Warning*

II. **Body**
   A. *Christians May Have Trials*
      1. "Heaviness through manifold temptations"
         a. Rejoicing is normal for us
         b. Testing times may cause discouragement
         c. We should remember these times are temporary
      2. Some Christians thought they were through with trials
         a. They thought faith in Christ would keep them from trials
         b. They thought the gospel train was the gravy train
      3. Then reality arrived
         a. In this world we have trouble (John 16:33)
         b. Christians are not immune from sickness
         c. Christians can have financial problems
         d. Christian parents can have trouble with their children
         e. Christian workers can have bosses who are hard to please
      4. These trials have not taken God by surprise
      5. He remains the same in all situations (Heb. 13:8)
   C. *Christians May Have Trials Related to Their Faith (v. 7)*
      1. "The trial of your faith"

2. How well Peter knew this
   a. Jesus had revealed His coming death on the cross
   b. Jesus had warned him to expect rejection by the world
   c. Peter had experienced persecution for his faith
3. Paul knew about these trials: imprisonment, stonings
4. Stephen knew about these trials: died as a martyr
5. James knew about these trials: finally died for his faith
6. Christians have had such trials through the centuries
7. Those who suffer for their faith are in good company

C. *Christians May Be Triumphant in Trials Through Their Savior (v. 8)*
   1. In trials our faith in Christ is being perfected
      a. It is like gold being purified by fire
      b. The return of Christ will reveal our faith is real
   2. Our victories through faith bring praise to Christ
   3. Our trials are all temporary
   4. Our rewards for faithfulness are all eternal
   5. Our unseen Savior goes through our trials with us
      a. He will never leave us nor forsake us (Heb. 13:5)
      b. His grace is sufficient for every trial (2 Cor. 12:9)

III. **Conclusion**
   A. *Are You Experiencing Trials?*
   B. *God Will Meet You in Your Trials and Enrich Your Faith*
   C. *Thank God for Trials That Bring You Closer to Him*

Faith for Family Crises

Faith Under Fire Series   *Matthew 15:21–28*

I. **Introduction**
   A. *Faith's Great Importance*
      1. Faith in Christ saves the soul
      2. Faith brings answers to prayer
      3. Faith drives away anxiety
      4. Faith pleases God
   B. *Faith's Greatest Test*
      1. When a loved one is afflicted
      2. Family crises drive us to our knees
   C. *Lessons from a Woman of Great Faith*

II. **Body**
   A. *The Dilemma of a Mother (v. 22)*
      1. "My daughter is grievously vexed with a devil"
         a. Mark says this was an unclean spirit
         b. The daughter controlled by unclean thoughts
         c. Probably suffered times of profane rage
      2. This gentile mother's prayer
         a. "Have mercy on me, O Lord, thou son of David"
         b. She accepted the deity of Christ
         c. She believed He could deliver her daughter
   B. *The Delay in the Lord's Answer (v. 23)*
      1. Here is faith under fire
         a. She cried out for help and the Lord was silent
         b. He was her only hope and He wasn't answering
      2. Has God seemed silent when you have prayed recently?
      3. This desperate woman kept on crying out for help
   C. *The Disgust of the Disciples (v. 23)*
      1. "Send her away"
      2. We may be bothered by those who have more faith than we do
      3. We may be annoyed by those who are more persistent in prayer
      4. Why the disciples wanted her sent away

  a. They wanted to get back to listening

  b. They didn't want to get involved

 D. *The Dimensions of the Woman's Faith*

  1. She was a gentile, a woman of Canaan

   a. She recognized Jesus as the Messiah

   b. She called Him Lord

  2. She believed Jesus was more powerful than the Devil

  3. She was able to see beyond seeming rejection

   a. He said He was sent only to Israel

   b. She responded: "Lord, help me"

  4. She understood Jesus better than His disciples

   a. She took the humble place

   b. "Dogs eat of the crumbs from their master's table"

   c. Her faith in Christ demanded she keep praying

III. Conclusion

 A. *The Lord Answered This Troubled Woman's Prayer*

  1. He saw her great faith and commended her

  2. Her daughter was released from the demon's power

  3. The miracle took place immediately

 B. *Faith Tested Under Fire Is Stronger in the Next Crisis*

 C. *Trust God to Answer Your Fervent, Persistent Prayer*

A Whale of a Thanksgiving

Faith Under Fire Series   *Jonah 2*

I.   Introduction
A.   *Great Times of Thanksgiving*
   1.   Israel's thanksgiving after deliverance from Egypt (Exod. 15)
   2.   Thanksgiving at the dedication of the temple (2 Chron. 5)
   3.   The first Thanksgiving in America
B.   *History's Most Unusual Thanksgiving*
   1.   Jonah giving thanks inside a big fish
   2.   He gives thanks and praise to God
   3.   Jonah had a whale of a Thanksgiving

II.   Body
A.   *This Thankful Man Was in a Dangerous Place*
   1.   How Jonah found himself in trouble
      a.   His call to go to Nineveh (ch. 1)
      b.   He fled from God in a ship heading for Tarshish
      c.   The great storm and the great fish
      d.   Jonah had thought his life was over
   2.   Thanksgiving follows deliverances from danger
      a.   This was true of the first Thanksgiving in America
      b.   The cold winter and sickness had claimed many lives
      c.   Encouragement came with a good harvest
      d.   It was time to give thanks
   3.   We live dangerous lives
      a.   Only a heartbeat from death
      b.   We are alive by God's grace
      c.   We have more than we deserve
   4.   We ought to be thankful
B.   *This Thankful Man Had Prayed a Desperate Prayer*
   1.   "I cried by reason of mine affliction" (v. 2)
   2.   Jonah cried out to God because he knew he was in trouble
   3.   We've all been in trouble

        a.   We were all lost in sin (Rom. 3:23)
        b.   We deserved nothing but death (Rom. 6:23)
        c.   God in love met us in our sins (John 3:16)
        d.   Christ died to pay for our sins (Rom. 5:8)
        e.   Salvation became available by faith (Rom. 10:9–10)

    4. We all ought to be thankful (Ps. 103)
    5. Some of us have been desperate over other problems
    6. We've prayed and God has delivered us
        a.   Our thanksgiving ought to reflect our deliverance
        b.   God has been good to us and we should give thanks

C. *This Thankful Man Had Nearly Given Up*
    1. "When my soul fainted within me"
    2. When discouraged he called on the Lord
        a.   He made vows to the Lord
        b.   He started giving thanks to the Lord
    3. God heard and rescued him
    4. God has heard our prayers and rescued us many times

III. Conclusion
    A. *We Are Alive Today and Should Be Thankful*
    B. *God Has Brought Us Safely to This Day*
    C. *Let's Have a Whale of a Thanksgiving*

Faith When All Your Castles Tumble

Faith Under Fire Series   *Job 1:21*

I. Introduction
   A. *Job's Happy Family*
   1. A good and godly prosperous man
   2. A great family: seven sons and three daughters
   3. Job was healthy and wealthy
   B. *The Day Job's Castles Tumbled*
   1. Enemies stole his oxen and killed those caring for them
   2. His sheep and shepherds were killed by lightning
   3. The Chaldeans stole his camels and killed their keepers
   4. His sons and daughters died in a storm
   C. *Job's Grief and Unshaken Faith*
   1. He tore his robe, shaved his head, and worshiped (v. 20)
   2. He declared his faith was still unshaken: "The LORD gave and the LORD hath taken away; blessed be the name of the LORD"
   3. How could Job do this?

II. Body
   A. *Job Saw the Lord As the Source of Life*
   1. "The LORD gave"
   2. Parents are but partners with God in giving life
   3. All life comes from the Lord
   4. Job knew the time he had with his children was by grace
      a. All the good times
      b. All the fun times
      c. All the family together times
   5. Every good and perfect gift is from above (James 1:17)
   6. God is the great giver: His greatest gift was His son
   B. *Job Saw the Lord As Sovereign over the Length of Life*
   1. "The Lord . . . hath taken away"
   2. Two surprising things about life

187

          a.   Its length when death seems near

          b.   Its brevity when the future seems sure

     3.   Our breath is in God's hands (Dan. 5:23)

     4.   Job understood that life is short at its longest

          a.   Childhood seems but yesterday to us all

          b.   It is important to be right with God at all times

     5.   Job didn't understand but his faith made him strong

C. *Job Saw the Lord As the Same No Matter What Happens in Life*

     1.   "Blessed be the name of the LORD"

     2.   It is easy to bless God when things are going well

     3.   Job was able to bless God when his castles tumbled

     4.   Job didn't understand so he spoke by faith

          a.   God had been faithful in the past

          b.   Why should he doubt the goodness of God now?

III. Conclusion

A. *God's Love Is Unchanging*

     1.   Have things gone badly for you?

     2.   God loves you in spite of your circumstances

B. *The Cross Proves God's Unchanging Love*

     1.   If you doubt God's love look at the cross

     2.   Christ died there for us because of His love

C. *God Loves You As You Are and Wants to Save You*

D. *Bring Your Sins and Broken Dreams to Him*

Faith When Funds Are Low

I.   Introduction

    A. *Getting to Know a Poor Widow of Jerusalem*
   1. Many things we don't know about her
      a. Her age, name, appearance, number of children
      b. The reason for her husband's death
   2. We know she was a woman of faith and very poor

    B. *Jesus Commended This Widow for Her Faith*
   1. His commendation has caused her to be remembered
   2. The favor of Christ endures
   3. The favor of the world passes away

    C. *Learning About a Poor Widow's Faith*

II. Body

    A. *The Widow's Faith Took Her to the Place of Worship (v. 1)*
   1. The treasury was at the temple in Jerusalem
   2. Some might have found excuses to stay away
      a. Clothes not good enough
      b. Too many wealthy people will be there
      c. Ashamed to go when unable to give a large gift
      d. Worked hard all week; too tired to go
      e. Rich members hadn't contributed to her needs
   3. She was poor, but rich in faith
   4. Her shortage of funds didn't keep her from the temple

    B. *The Widow's Faith Moved Her to Give (v. 2)*
   1. Many would have thought they couldn't afford to give
      a. Every penny was needed for living
      b. Let the wealthy do the giving
   2. She considered giving an act of worship
   3. Christian giving has spiritual significance
   4. She couldn't give much but couldn't keep from giving
      a. She gave two mites (small copper coins)

      b.   Her gift must have seemed insignificant to the rest

      c.   It was an important gift to the widow

      d.   She wanted to do something for the Lord

C. *The Widow's Faith Caused Her to Give All She Had (v. 4)*

   1.   Jesus saw this as the largest gift of the day

      a.   He said she gave more than the rest

      b.   God measures our gifts by our ability to give

   2.   The others gave part of their wealth

   3.   The widow held nothing back

      a.   Imagine the inward struggle about this gift

      b.   She would have nothing left

      c.   Faith still moved her to give it all

   4.   Faith giving is revealed by what we keep

III. **Conclusion**

A. *Message on a Gravestone in England*

        What I spent, I had

        What I saved, I lost

        What I gave, I have

B. *God Is the Great Giver*

   1.   He gave His Son

   2.   He gives eternal life to those who receive Christ

C. *Faith Receives God's Good Gifts*

D. *Faith Gives to God Even When Funds Are Low*

Faith When Others Are Against Us

Faith Under Fire Series Ends   *Daniel 6*

I. Introduction
    A. *From Young Captive to President*
        1. Daniel and friends captives of Nebuchadnezzar in Babylon
            a. Choosing to reject the king's food and wine (1:8)
            b. Daniel interpreting Nebuchadnezzar's dreams (chs. 2 & 4)
        2. Daniel predicts Belshazzar's death (ch. 5)
        3. Darius, the Mede, appoints Daniel top President (ch. 6)
        4. Kings and kingdoms fall; God's servants continue
    B. *Darius Saw That Daniel Was Different (v. 3)*
        1. The king sensed an excellent spirit in Daniel
        2. The king made Daniel top man
    C. *The Plot Thickens*

II. Body
    A. *People of Faith Are Not Always Popular (v. 4)*
        1. The other princes and presidents despised Daniel
        2. Serving God has always been costly
            a. Prophets were often ignored and jailed or stoned
            b. John the Baptist was jailed and beheaded
            c. Paul was jailed and martyred
            d. All of the Apostles martyred except John, who was exiled
        3. Jesus warned His disciples of rejection by the world (John 15)
        4. Christians have suffered for their faith for centuries
        5. Will your faith hold up under persecution?
    B. *The Presidents and Princes and Their Plot (vv. 4–9)*
        1. Daniel's enemies searched for a flaw in him
            a. They could find no fault in him
            b. What a credit to this faithful man
            c. Reminds us of Pilate's conclusion about Jesus: "I find no fault in Him"

   2. The only opening for Daniel's enemies
       a. He was a man of faith
       b. He was a man of prayer
       c. They would find a way to prosecute him for
           praying
   3. The infamous decree that sent Daniel to the lion's
       den
       a. Petitions only to the king for thirty days
       b. They knew Daniel would keep petitioning God
       c. Their wicked plot would sentence him to death
   C. *Faith Always Finds Help in Prayer (vv. 10–28)*
       1. Daniel's response to the king's decree
           a. He kept on praying as before
           b. Prayed with his windows open: not in secret
       2. Darius sent Daniel to the lion's den
           a. The king had confidence in Daniel's prayers
           b. He believed God would deliver him (v. 16)
       3. God protected Daniel from the hungry lions
           a. He millenialized the lions for a night
           b. The king spent the night fasting and so did the
               lions

III. Conclusion

   A. *Triumph Follows Trials*
       1. Daniel's angelic guest in the lion's den (v. 22)
       2. The mouths of the lions were shut
   B. *The King Calls for His People to Turn to the Lord
       (vv. 26–27)*
   C. *Faith Proving True Under Fire Impacts Others for
       Christ*

The Virgin Birth of Christ

The Birth of Christ Series Begins   *Isaiah 7:14*

I. **Introduction**
    A. *The Birth of Christ*
        1. The central subject of the Bible
        2. The Old Testament prophecies it
        3. The New Testament proclaims it
    B. *The Virgin Birth of Christ*
        1. How can it be true?
        2. Must Christians accept it?
    C. *What Shall We Think About the Virgin Birth of Christ?*

II. **Body**
    A. *The Virgin Birth Is a Must If You Accept the Bible*
        1. The Bible tells us of the virgin birth (Isa. 7:14)
        2. The Promised One was to be the seed of the woman (Gen. 3:15)
        3. Gabriel told Mary of the coming virgin birth (Luke 1:26–38)
        4. The angel of the Lord told Joseph (Matt. 1:18–24)
        5. Matthew assures us Christ was virgin born (Matt. 1:25)
        6. Paul declares Christ was made of a woman (Gal. 4:4)
        7. Christ the only begotten son of God (John 3:16; 3:18)
    B. *The Virgin Birth Is a Miracle You Accept by Faith (Luke 1:37)*
        1. The Bible says it; we believe it; that settles it
        2. Mary had to accept this miracle by faith
            a. She had difficulty understanding it
            b. "How shall this be seeing a man I know not?" (Luke 1:34)
            c. Nothing is impossible with God (Luke 1:37)
        3. God formed the first man from the dust of the ground
        4. Why then should the virgin birth be hard to accept?
        5. Other miracles we accept
            a. The opening of the Red Sea

b. Manna provided for the Israelites
c. Water flowing from a rock for thirsty thousands

6. The miracle of the virgin birth is well within God's power

C. *The Virgin Birth Is an Unacceptable Mystery Until You Accept Christ As Your Savior (1 Cor. 2:14)*

1. Do you find it impossible to accept this miracle?
2. Try accepting the following:
    a. Christ feeding five thousand with a few loaves and fish
    b. Christ walking on the Sea of Galilee
    c. Christ stilling the sea during a storm
    d. Christ raising the dead
    e. Christ rising from the dead
3. The miracles of Christ are unacceptable until you accept Him
4. Paul explains your problem (1 Cor. 2:14):
    a. You are trying to understand things of the Spirit
    b. This is impossible until you have the Holy Spirit
    c. Receive Christ as Savior and your eyes will be opened
    d. The virgin birth will not be hard to accept anymore

III. Conclusion

A. *The God of Miracles Loves You*
B. *Respond to His Love and Come to Him As a Sinner*
C. *Receive Christ As Savior by Faith (Acts 16:31)*
D. *The Miracle of New Birth Will Take Place in You*

The Magnificat

The Birth of Christ Series   *Luke 1:46–56*

I. **Introduction**
   A. *Mary Meets an Angel*
      1. Gabriel: bearer of glad tidings
      2. The greatest news ever delivered: the Savior to be born
   B. *Mary's Response to Gabriel*
      1. She was troubled (v. 29)
      2. Gabriel told her not to be afraid (v. 30)
      3. She was confused: "How shall this be?"
   C. *Mary Is Told to Expect a Miracle*
      1. "The power of the Highest shall overshadow thee" (v. 35)
      2. "For with God nothing shall be impossible" (v. 37)
   D. *Mary Begins to Rejoice (vv. 46–55)*

II. **Body**
   A. *Mary Rejoicing in Her Personal Savior (vv. 46–48)*
      1. "My spirit hath rejoiced in God my Savior"
      2. Mary's great heritage and spiritual experiences
         a. The line of David
         b. The purity of her life
         c. Her meeting with Gabriel
         d. Elizabeth's salutation
      3. Still, she takes her place as one who needs a Savior
         a. A Savior for us all is the greatest cause to rejoice
         b. Do you join Mary as one who needs a Savior?
         c. Will you accept Him by faith today?
   B. *Mary Rejoices in the Personality of Her Savior (vv. 48–53)*
      1. Have you praised God today for who He is?
      2. Consider Mary's reasons to praise Him
         a. Mary's praise for His love (v. 48)
         b. Mary's praise for His favor (v. 48)
         c. Mary's praise for His might (v. 49)
         d. Mary's praise for His mercy (v. 50)
         e. Mary's praise for His grace (v. 52)
         f. Mary's praise for His goodness (v. 53)

       3. What are your reasons to rejoice in your Lord?

   C. *Mary Rejoicing in the Promises of God (vv. 54–55)*

       1. God had helped Israel

       2. God had been merciful to Israel

       3. God had kept His promises to Abraham

       4. The coming of the Savior was one of these promises

       5. Promises about the Savior Mary would see fulfilled

          a. He would be born of a virgin

          b. He would be born in Bethlehem

          c. He would die for sinners

          d. He would rise again

       6. God keeps His promises

       7. He will keep His promises to you and me

III. **Conclusion**

   A. *Are You Rejoicing in the Savior?*

   B. *Consider What He Has Done for Us All*

   C. *It's Time to Rejoice!*

When the Sunrise of Heaven Visited Earth

The Birth of Christ Series   *Luke 1:78–79*

I. **Introduction**
   A. *Gabriel's Two Important Missions*
      1. To Zacharias: announcing John the Baptist would be born
      2. To Mary: announcing Jesus would be born
   B. *Mary and Elisabeth Together for Three Months of Waiting*
   C. *John Is Born and Zacharias Prophesies*
      1. John the Baptist to prepare the way for Jesus
      2. Jesus called the "dayspring from on high" (v. 78)
      3. What does this mean to us?

II. **Body**
   A. *Christ Gives Light to Those in Darkness (v. 79)*
      1. "To give light to them that sit in darkness"
      2. Dayspring is a poetic name for dawn or sunrise
      3. Christ came dispelling the darkness of this world
      4. God always brings light out of darkness
         a. In creation: "Let there be light" (Gen. 1:3)
         b. In salvation: "the light of the world" (John 8:12)
         c. In walking with God: "as he is in the light"(1 John 1:7)
      5. Jesus came to bring light into our lives
   B. *Christ Gives Light to Those in the Shadow of Death*
      1. "To give light to them that sit in the shadow of death"
      2. We all live in the shadow of death (Heb. 9:27)
         a. We are but a heartbeat from eternity
         b. An atheist said: "Now for a fearful leap into the dark"
      3. The death and resurrection of Christ changed this
         a. The open tomb removed darkness from death
         b. Sun shining into that tomb lighted death for us all
      4. Jesus overcame death at every meeting
         a. The daughter of Jairus

197

   b. The son of the widow of Nain

   c. His friend Lazarus

  5. He overcame death for you and me

 C. *Christ Gives Light to Those Who Need Direction*
   (v. 79)

  1. "To guide our feet into the way of peace"

  2. Walking through this dark world we need a guide

   a. Jesus is that guide

   b. He lights a way for our feet

   c. He guides our feet into the way of peace

  3. "Peace": what a good word

   a. Is peace more than a word to you?

   b. Have you found peace?

  4. Jesus wants to give you lasting peace

III. Conclusion

 A. *What Does the Birth of Christ Mean to You?*

  1. Is Jesus just a reason for the season?

  2. Is Christmas just another religious holiday?

 B. *Christ Wants to Bring You Light and Life*

  1. Light for your darkness

  2. Light when death's shadow falls across your way

  3. Light to guide you from earth to heaven

The Night of Miracles

The Birth of Christ Series   *Luke 2:1–20*

I. Introduction

   A. *All of History Had Been Moving Toward That Night*

      1. All the roads of Scripture wound toward Bethlehem

      2. Mary and Joseph had come only from Nazareth

         a. But the ages had been waiting for them to arrive

         b. Micah had said they would be there (Micah 5:2)

   B. *A Night of Miracles Had Long Been on Heaven's Calendar*

      1. Angels looked forward to their appointments

      2. Words of the prophets awaited fulfillment

      3. The baby in Mary's womb would soon light up the night

   C. *What Were the Miracles of Christmas?*

II. Body

   A. *The Miracle of the Humble Birth (vv. 1–7)*

      1. Christ comes down from heaven to a stable

         a. He enters the world from the womb of a virgin

         b. It is this baby's world

         c. It was made by Him (John 1:10)

         d. He has come down to redeem it

         e. His world will reject Him

      2. Consider the contrasts of His condescension

         a. From the fragrance of heaven to the stench of the stable

         b. From the worship of angels to rejection by the innkeeper

         c. From the songs of the saints to the braying of donkeys

         d. From a robe of royalty to wrappings of rags

         e. From a mansion in heaven to a manger on earth

      3. He came down to save you and me

   B. *The Miracle of the Heavenly Hosts (vv. 8–14)*

      1. Angels have been busy since the fullness of time has come

          a.   Gabriel has visited Zacharias and Mary
          b.   The angel of the Lord has advised Joseph in a dream
    2.   Now angels will carry their message to Judean hillsides
          a.   Where Rachel's tomb was located
          b.   Where Samuel had anointed David to be king
          c.   Where Ruth had gleaned in the fields of Boaz
    3.   Shepherds must be notified of the Savior's birth
    4.   The heavenly chorus will sing of peace on earth
    5.   This is a miracle night: a night to remember

  C. *The Miracle of God's Work in the Hearts of Men (vv. 15–20)*
    1.   The Roman Empire and its taxing-census
          a.   Joseph and Mary must be brought to Bethlehem
          b.   Empires are easily moved to fulfill God's will
          c.   Prophecy must be fulfilled (Micah 5:2)
    2.   Shepherds will become evangelists
    3.   Wise men will journey far following a star
    4.   The actors in this drama of the ages are in place
    5.   Christ is born: the greatest miracle of all

III. Conclusion
  A. *Miracles Will Continue*
    1.   Like the shepherds, many will come to Jesus
    2.   Like the wise men, many will worship him
  B. *Have You Become One of the Miracles of Christmas?*
  C. *Your Miracle Awaits*
  D. *Come in Faith to Jesus and Know the Miracle of His Salvation*

Herod: The Enemy of Christ

The Birth of Christ Series Ends   *Matthew 2:1–19*

I. **Introduction**
   A. *The Character of Christmas We Miss*
      1. One we would rather omit
      2. How often have you heard Herod's name at Christmas?
   B. *Heaven's Focus Is Different*
      1. Cattle upstage the king
      2. A stable gains world attention instead of the palace
      3. Actors at Christmas dress like shepherds, not like Herod
   C. *The King Does Have a Part to Play in This Drama*
      1. He tries to deceive the wise men
      2. He wants to destroy Christ
   D. *How Herod Became the Villain of Christmas*

II. **Body**
   A. *Herod and His Troubled Heart (v. 3)*
      1. The wise men arrive at Herod's palace
         a. They explain their mission
         b. They seek help in finding the King of the Jews
      2. Herod is troubled
         a. He fears he will lose control
         b. He fears Christ will become king
         c. Are you afraid to lose control of your life?
         d. Are you afraid to allow Christ to be king?
      3. Herod in contrast to the wise men
         a. The wise men worship and Herod worries
         b. The wise give and Herod groans
         c. The wise men praise and Herod plots
   B. *Herod Brings Trouble to Others (vv. 3–18)*
      1. "All Jerusalem with him"
      2. When you reject Christ it affects others
         a. No one lives or dies to himself (Rom. 14:7)
         b. What we do brings heartache or blessing to others
      3. Herod is upset and this upsets the city
      4. The terrible temper of a troubled man

201

a.   Herod's slaughter of the children of Bethlehem
b.   Where angels sang, mothers weep
c.   The place of glory became a place of grief
5.   Bring your troubled heart to Jesus
6.   He will meet you in your trouble and give you peace

C.   *Herod in Trouble Forever (v. 19)*
1.   "But when Herod was dead"
2.   Herod died in his sins
a.   He went from suffering to suffering
b.   Herod, in hell, is still troubled
3.   What Herod missed
a.   Christ came to save but Herod died lost
b.   Christ came to cleanse but Herod died guilty
c.   Christ came to give peace but Herod died troubled

III.   Conclusion

A.   *Are You Like Herod or the Wise Men?*
B.   *Those Who Reject Jesus Never Find Peace*
C.   *Wise Ones Still Seek and Worship Jesus*

Our Lord the Leveler

Luke 3:4–6

I. Introduction

A. *The Miraculous Birth of John the Baptist*
   1. Zacharias and Elisabeth had long wanted a child
   2. Gabriel let them know their prayers were answered
   3. John was born to prepare the way for Christ (Isa. 40)

B. *Thirty Years Have Passed*

C. *The Moment for John to Begin His Ministry Arrives*
   1. Sharing one of John's sermons
   2. What can we learn from it?

II. Body

A. *Every Valley Shall Be Filled . . . Exalted (v. 5)*
   1. What does this mean?
      a. Too graphic to be geographic
      b. God is no bulldozer driver
      c. This has to do with life
   2. Fitting that John starts with valleys
      a. Meeting the lowly first
      b. Letting them know God will lift them up
   3. Bible examples
      a. The woman at the well was in a valley
      b. Blind Bartimaeus was in a valley
      c. Mary Magdalene was in a valley
      d. Our Lord saved and exalted them all
   4. Your need makes you eligible for God's grace

B. *Every Mountain and Hill Shall Be Brought Low (v. 5)*
   1. The proud must be humbled to be helped
   2. Consider the Pharisee and the Publican
   3. This speaks of the need of the rich young ruler
   4. The problem of pride is as old as Satan (Isa. 14:12–15)
   5. How pride may keep you from salvation
      a. You don't see yourself as a sinner
      b. You think you are good enough for heaven
      c. You would never respond to a gospel invitation
      d. Your pride keeps you from being blessed

      6. Let every mountain and hill in your life be brought low

      7. Get rid of pride and humbly come to Jesus

  C. *The Crooked Shall Be Made Straight (v. 5)*

      1. How devious the sinful mind of man

         a. He lies, he cheats, he steals

         b. He is dishonest in his business

      2. God has straightened out many crooked ones

      3. Those who trust in Christ are made new (2 Cor. 5:17)

  D. *The Rough Ways Shall Be Made Smooth (v. 5)*

      1. Christ has made many rough ones smooth

      2. Cursing, swearing Peter became the spokesman for the church

      3. Tongues that blasphemed have become tongues that bless

      4. Jesus specializes in making the rough ones smooth

III. Conclusion

  A. *Jesus Wants to Meet You Where You Are*

  B. *He Will Change You from What You Are to What You Should Be*

  C. *Come to Him in Faith and Find All Things New*

Jesus Wants to Be Your Friend

John 15:13–15

I. Introduction
- A. *A Sermon for Friend Sunday*
    1. Some here because invited by friends
    2. Good friends invite others to church and to Jesus
- B. *What Is a Friend?*
    1. Dictionary: "One who is personally well known and for whom one has warm regard or affection"
    2. A friend is one who knows your faults and loves you
- C. *Why Jesus Wants to Be Your Friend*

II. Body
- A. *Jesus Loves You (v. 13)*
    1. The Bible says Jesus loves you (John 3:16)
    2. The children's song of love is true:
        - a. "Jesus loves me this I know
        - b. For the Bible tells me so"
    3. Our Lord's unfailing love
        - a. He loves when others forsake (Heb. 13:15)
        - b. He loves in spite of our sins (1 Tim. 1:15)
    4. The cross proves His love
        - a. "Greater love hath no man than this"
        - b. He laid down His life for us (John 10:11)
- B. *Jesus Will Accept You As You Are (v. 13)*
    1. God loved us while we were sinners (Rom. 5:8)
        - a. Loved us while we were enemies (Rom. 5:10)
        - b. Died to make us His friends (1 John 1:7)
    2. Nothing to change before coming to Him
    3. "Just As I Am" is true
    4. Are you afraid God won't forgive your sins?
        - a. Jesus didn't come to rub them in
        - b. He came to rub them out (Isa. 44:22–23)
- C. *Jesus Wants to Be with You Forever (v. 13)*
    1. Friends want to be together
        - a. They enjoy fellowship
        - b. They have things in common
    2. Promises about His eternal fellowship

        a. "I am with you alway" (Matt. 28:20)
        b. "I will never leave thee" (Heb. 13:5)
        c. " . . . nor forsake thee" (Heb. 13:5)
    3. Jesus wants you to be with Him in heaven
       (John 14:1–3)
        a. He is preparing places for His friends
        b. Prepared places for prepared people
        c. Are you prepared?
    4. "So shall we ever be with the Lord"
       (1 Thess. 4:17)
    5. Heaven will compensate for trials here
       (Rev. 7:15–17)

III. Conclusion

    A. *What a Friend We Have in Jesus!*
    B. *Is He Your Friend?*
    C. *Accept This Heavenly Friend Today*
       1. Come to Him as you are (Matt. 11:28)
       2. Receive Him by faith (Rom. 5:1)
       3. He'll be your Friend forever (John 3:16)

Looking for Rain

1 Kings 18:1, 41–46

I. Introduction

A. *Meet Elijah: Mighty Prophet of God*
1. The man who did not die (2 Kings 2:11)
2. Elijah at the Transfiguration (Matt. 17:3)
3. His coming tribulation ministry (Rev. 11)

B. *Elijah Prophecies a Drought (17:1)*
1. Tells King Ahab it isn't going to rain
2. Elijah had prayed for this drought (James 5:17–18)
3. Ahab and Israel had forsaken the Lord

II. Body

A. *The Drought Is to End (v. 1)*
1. The drought had brought a famine
2. Elijah preserved during the famine
   a. Preserved at the brook Cherith (17:2–7)
   b. Preserved by a widow (17:9–16)
   c. God's provision is unaffected by drought (Phil 4:19)
3. Droughts are times for decisions (18:21)
4. God is unchanged in times of drought (Heb. 13:8)
   a. Physical difficulties do not change God
   b. Spiritual difficulties do not change God
   c. He loves us in times of drought (Rom. 8:38–39)

B. *The Demonstration of God's Power (vv. 21–38)*
1. Elijah calls for a contest
   a. His challenge on Mt. Carmel
   b. The God who answers by fire
2. The Prophets of Baal cry out in vain
   a. They prayed all morning (v. 26)
   b. Prayed enthusiastically: leaping on the altar
   c. Prayed sacrificially: cutting themselves
   d. Prayed until evening *but no answer came*
3. Elijah prepares to pray
   a. He repairs the altar of the Lord (v. 30)
   b. Digs a trench around the altar (v. 32)
   c. The trench filled water (vv. 33–35)
   d. The value of preparing to pray in faith

      4.   Elijah's brief prayer (vv. 36–37)

      5.   The fire of the Lord fell (v. 38)

      6.   We need to have that fire fall again

  C. *The Drenching Rain (vv. 41–46)*

      1.   The sound of abundance of rain (v. 41)

      2.   Elijah sends his weatherman to scan the sky

         a.   Not a cloud to be seen (v. 43)

         b.   "Go again seven times" (v. 43)

         c.   Elijah expected God to answer his prayer

      3.   A cloud the size of a man's hand (v. 44)

         a.   That was all Elijah needed

         b.   He knew rain was coming

III.   Conclusion

  A. *Let's Expect the Spiritual Drought to End*

  B. *Let's Look for the First Signs of Revival*

  C. *Let's Rejoice in What God Will Do in Our Lives*

Questions to Quell the Fear of Witnessing

Acts 1:4–11

I. Introduction
A. *Witnessing: the Greatest Lack in Churches Today*
1. We do many things well: services, projects, etc.
2. Programs have become almost professional
3. But few churches excel in witnessing

B. *Fear Holds Many Back from Sharing Their Faith*
1. We fear the response of people
2. We fear public opinion

C. *Three Questions to Fight Our Fears*

II. Body
A. *What Time Is It? (vv. 4–7)*
1. Anticipation at the ascension of Jesus
   a. Sins had been paid for at the cross
   b. Christ had risen as He said
   c. Now for the Kingdom?
2. "Lord, wilt thou at this time?"
3. Many have longed to know the time
   a. Date setters have failed to discover it
   b. The sacred secret (Matt. 24:36)
4. But we know what time it is:
   a. It is time to witness
   b. It is time to win souls
   c. Each day brings us closer to Christ's return
5. This urgency should overcome our fears of witnessing

B. *Who Empowers Us? (v. 8)*
1. "Ye shall receive power"
   a. This power to come from the Holy Spirit
   b. The Holy Spirit to come at Pentecost
2. The promise was fulfilled
   a. The Holy Spirit came (Acts 2)
   b. Thousands were saved
3. Great News: the Holy Spirit Is Still Here
   a. He lives within each believer (1 Cor. 6:19)
   b. His power is not diminished
   c. We are to witness in His power

    4. The Holy Spirit prepares hearts for our witness
    5. The Holy Spirit provides words for witnessing
    6. Why should we fear when the Holy Spirit is here?

  C. *Who Has Called Us to Witness? (v. 8)*
    1. "Witnesses unto me"
    2. Jesus, Himself, has called us to witness
      a. The One who endured the cross for us
      b. The One who arose from the grave
      c. The Man of tears and compassion
      d. The One who is coming again
      e. The One who will reward His servants
    3. More fearful to disobey than to witness

III. Conclusion

  A. *Exchange Your Fears for Faith*
  B. *Start Witnessing Now*
    1. In view of our Lord's return
    2. In the power of the Holy Spirit
    3. In obedience to our Savior

Getting Peace about Witnessing

Philippians 4:6–9

I. Introduction

A. *Fear Is an Enemy of Us All*
   1. Fear: the first evidence of the fall (Gen. 3:10)
   2. Fear keeps many from salvation
      a. Afraid God doesn't love them
      b. Afraid their sins are too serious to be forgiven
      c. Afraid of public opinion
B. *Fear Keeps Many Believers from Witnessing*
   1. Afraid to tell others of Christ
   2. Afraid to give out tracts
   3. Afraid to invite others to church
C. *Replacing Fear with Faith for Witnessing*

II. Body

A. *We Must Pray About Witnessing (v. 6)*
   1. "In everything by prayer"
   2. We pray about many things:
      a. Physical problems, finances, family needs
      b. The church, the government
   3. When did you last pray about witnessing?
   4. Pray for God to lead us to needy souls
   5. Pray for the right words
   6. Pray for people to be saved
B. *We Must Have a Plan for Witnessing (vv. 6–7)*
   1. This text gives a plan for peace
      a. Be anxious for nothing
      b. Pray about everything
      c. Give thanks for God's blessings
   2. It is right to have a plan
      a. God is organized; has a plan (consider creation)
      b. We need a plan for witnessing
   3. A good plan for witnessing
      a. Be alert to needs of those you meet
      b. Be compassionate to those in need
      c. Use tracts that focus on needs
      d. Share your testimony

211

C. *We Must Be Positive in Our Witnessing (v. 8)*
    1. "Think on these things"
    2. Expect results from your witnessing
    3. Believe people need your witness
    4. Trust God to produce fruit from your witnessing
       a. Lost people coming to Christ
       b. Troubled people finding peace
       c. Backsliders returning to the Father

D. *We Must Proceed with Our Witnessing (v. 9)*
    1. " . . . and seen in me, do"
    2. Good intentions are not enough
    3. The more we witness the less we fear to witness
    4. Just do it

III. Conclusion

A. *As Faith Increases Fear Decreases*
B. *Working Your Plan Brings Results*
C. *Obedience in Witnessing Brings Peace*

Sanctified Scattering

I. Introduction

   A. Words for Worship and Witnessing
     1. Gather to worship
     2. Scatter to evangelize
   B. Your Presence Shows You Value Worship
     1. You're here to sing, to pray, to praise, to learn
     2. What will you do when you scatter?
     3. God values your worship and your witnessing
   C. Early Christians Were Scattered by Persecution

II. Body

   A. When Scattered, They Didn't Agonize
     1. They could have groaned about many things
       a. Believed and trouble came
       b. Gave sacrificially and became poor
       c. Gave love and received hatred
       d. Leaders were jailed and martyred
     2. They kept praising in adversity
       a. The world wondered at them
       b. Their enemy (Saul) became one of them
   B. When Scattered, They Didn't Criticize
     1. They might have blamed their leaders
       a. "If you hadn't been so dogmatic"
       b. "If you hadn't angered the public"
       c. "If you had been more diplomatic"
     2. Criticism cripples churches today
       a. Criticism of leaders
       b. Criticism of each other
     3. Negativism robs believers of their power
   C. When Scattered, They Didn't Politicize
     1. The early church had no political agenda
       a. Their goal was preaching the Gospel
       b. Changing their world one person at a time
     2. The early church had no political power
       a. No evidence they desired it
       b. No marches on Rome
       c. No rebellion against leaders

    3. Dangers when churches choose a political message
       a. Historically this has been disastrous
       b. Exchanges an eternal message for a temporal one
       c. Political blunders reflect on the church
    4. "Render unto Caesar" (Matt. 22:21)
    5. "My kingdom is not of this world" (John 18:36)
  D. *When Scattered, They Evangelized*
    1. "Went everywhere preaching the Word"
    2. People are lost everywhere we go (Rom. 3:23)
    3. People need Jesus everywhere we go (Acts 4:12)
    4. We are to evangelize everywhere we go (Acts 1:8)

III. Conclusion
  A. *What Will We Do When Scattered?*
    1. Agonize? Criticize? Politicize?
    2. Let's evangelize
  B. *How Many Will We Reach for Christ This Week?*

Three Hundred Heroes

Judges 6–7

I. **Introduction**
  A. *Midian Became Israel's Oppressor (Jud. 6:1–6)*
    1. God allows His people to be temporarily oppressed
    2. Seven years of chastening for their sins (Judges 6:1)
      a. Living in dens and caves
      b. Israel's harvests destroyed
  B. *The Choosing and Commissioning of Gideon (Judges 6:7–40)*
    1. An angel appears to Gideon (v. 12)
      a. Gideon's surprise and his doubts (vv. 12–15)
      b. Gideon seeks signs (vv. 17–40)
    2. Gideon prepared to lead a tiny army of heroes
  C. *Why God Chose Gideon's Three Hundred Heroes*

II. **Body**
  A. *They Were Courageous Men (v. 3)*
    1. "Whosoever is fearful"
      a. Fear is the opposite of faith
      b. Courage and faith are friends
    2. Courage and faith in the life of Joshua
      a. "Be strong and very courageous" (Josh. 1:6–7)
      b. "Be strong and of a good courage" (Josh. 1:9)
    3. The psalmist's call for courage (Ps. 27:14)
    4. Paul's courage in trials (Acts 28:15)
    5. Courage and the Christian life
      a. It takes courage to confront the Tempter
      b. It takes courage to witness
      c. It takes courage to do right
      d. It takes courage to stand alone
    6. Christ the supreme example of courage
    7. These men stayed when 22,000 were afraid
  B. *They Were Careful Men (vv. 6–7)*
    1. A strange test to be in Gideon's army
      a. Choosing those who lap water like a dog
      b. Rejecting those who bow down to drink
    2. The majority (9,700) plunged their faces into the water

215

        a.   More concerned with water than watching
        b.   Quenching their thirst more important than victory
    3.   Three hundred lifted the water in their hands
        a.   Lapped and looked at the same time
        b.   Watching more important than water
    4.   Good soldiers are careful
        a.   We are in a life or death struggle
        b.   Our enemy is crafty and strong

C. *They Were Committed Men (vv. 8–22)*
    1.   They were committed to Gideon
        a.   Stayed with him when others left
        b.   Didn't fear being a minority
    2.   They were committed to God
        a.   Accepted their strange weapons
        b.   Expected to win with trumpets, pitchers, and lamps

III.   Conclusion
A. *Vance Havner and Gideon's Men: "Every revival begins with a Gideon's band, a core of effectives, the church within the church"*
B. *A Call for Courageous, Careful, Committed Christian Soldiers*

The Man Who Walked with God

Genesis 5:24

I. **Introduction**
   A. *A Stroll through the Cemetery*
      1. A chapter of life and death
      2. Gems among the genealogies
         a. Adam and Eve had sons and daughters
         b. Methuselah: the oldest man ever
         c. The birth of Noah
         d. Enoch: the man who did not die
   B. *Learning More about This Unusual Man*

II. **Body**
   A. *Enoch Walked with God*
      1. When did this walk begin?
      2. What factors led to faith?
         a. His observation of death?
         b. His observation of nature?
         c. Revelation handed down from Adam?
            (1) Things Adam learned in Eden
            (2) Abel's continuing testimony (Heb. 11:4)
         d. When he became a father (v. 22)?
      3. God reveals Himself to those who long to walk with Him
   B. *Enoch Did Not Die (Heb. 11:4)*
      1. The recurring phrase in Gen. 5: "And he died"
      2. Enoch was translated: didn't "see death"
      3. Light in a dark chapter
      4. Life in a chapter of death
      5. Enoch pictures the church at the rapture
         a. "We shall not all sleep" (1 Cor. 15:51)
         b. "Alive and remain" (1 Thess. 4:15)
         c. We may never die
   C. *Enoch Was a Prophet (Jude 14–15)*
      1. He prophesied Christ would come
      2. A clear description of the return of Christ
         a. Christ coming with His saints (Rev. 19–20)
         b. Christ coming to set up His kingdom
         c. Christ coming to bring judgment

      3. Enoch knew sin did not pay (v. 15)
         a. Preached against ungodly deeds
         b. Preached against ungodly words

III. **Conclusion**
    A. *Enoch's Role in the Future*
      1. Perhaps one of the witnesses of Rev. 11
      2. His message will be the same (Jude 14–15)
      3. He may return to prophesy and die (Heb. 9:27)
      4. Translated to be a Tribulation prophet
    B. *Have You Begun the Walk of Faith?*
    C. *Those Who Walk with God Below Will Walk with Him Above*

Back to Bethel

Genesis 35:1–3

I. **Introduction**
- A. *Jacob and His Troubles*
  1. A son of Isaac, a patriarch of Israel
  2. He deceived Esau and their father (Gen. 25–27)
  3. Fled to Canaan to escape Esau
- B. *Jacob at Bethel (Gen. 28:10–22)*
  1. On Jacob's way to Canaan, God met him
  2. The ladder from earth to heaven
  3. Jacob named the place "Bethel" (the House of God)
- C. *Returning to Bethel*

II. **Body**
- A. *The Call to Jacob to Go Back to Bethel (v. 1)*
  1. This is a call from God
  2. God calls wanderers to return
     - a. He calls us back to places of dedication
     - b. He calls us to return to Him
  3. Jacob at Bethel the first time (Gen. 28:10–22)
     - a. He had stopped to rest
     - b. He heard God speak to him
     - c. Heaven and earth were joined
     - d. God's promises became real
     - e. God promised to be with him
     - f. He made vows to God
  4. God calls us back to places of commitment
- B. *The Conviction That Caused Jacob to Go Back to Bethel (v. 2)*
  1. Conviction brought action
     - a. "Put away the strange Gods"
     - b. "Be clean"
     - c. "Change your garments"
  2. Strange things in the lives of believers
     - a. Strange plans
     - b. Strange attitudes
     - c. Strange words
     - d. Strange goals

3. Are you convicted about the strange things in your life?
C. *The Consecration of Jacob's Heart As He Returns to Bethel*
    1. "Let us arise and go"
    2. Even better than the prodigal's resolution
        a. "I will arise and go" is personal
        b. "Let us arise and go" is public
    3. Consecration made Jacob worship: he built an altar
    4. Consecration made Jacob faithful:
        a. Said God had answered his prayer
        b. Remembered God had been with him

III.   Conclusion
A. *The Impact of Jacob's Return to Bethel*
B. *Come Back to Your Bethel*
    1. On his family: gave up their gods and gold
    2. On the community: his enemies feared him
    1. God is calling you back to your Bethel
    2. Responding will impact others for God

Scripture Index